Contents

Chapter 1. Advanced Force Operations

Chapter 2. Ugly Baby to Operation Viking Hammer

Chapter 3. Operation Viking Hammer

Chapter 4. The Green Line

Chapter 5. Introspections (footnotes)

This book is dedicated to my wife, my family, and the men of ODA-081, circa 2003

This content in this book was approved by the DoD Prepublication Review Process

Introduction

Operation Viking Hammer (OVH) took place in Northeastern Iraqi Kurdistan on March 28th, 2003 in an area east of the village of Halabja. The focus of the operation was to defeat Ansar Al Islam (AAI) and secure the "Sargat Chemical Facility." OVH was one of the largest Unconventional Warfare operations in Special Forces history. There were 6 Green Beret teams, a handful of CIA Ground Branch operatives, a few Air Force Special Tactics Squadron operators, and roughly 8000 Kurdish Peshmerga from the Patriotic Union of Kurdistan (PUK). No conventional forces were involved. Three Silver Stars were earned by my team Captain, Team Sergeant, and our Communications Sergeant. Some of the CIA and Air Force operators also received high level awards for valor. For what it's worth, I was recommended for a Silver Star, but it got downgraded to a Bronze Star with V device.

OVH was unique. It was a singular objective that was taken by means of a deliberate, unified attack against an entrenched enemy. We didn't ride horses, and it wasn't on the news. OVH was a significant emotional event that I will never forget. Moreover, the Advanced Force Operations prior to the war in Northern Iraq that preceded OVH (chapter one) were also very important, and a once-in-a-generation type of mission for a career Green Beret.

For historical context, OVH was part of a larger strategy in three basic ways. First, as I mentioned, OVH was intended to "take out" AAI, an Islamic extremist group that had taken over a large area along the Iranian border in Northern Iraq. Removing AAI (and two other extremist groups) was intended to secure the "rear" of the northern front once our effort shifted to fighting against the Iraqi military. Second, OVH had the possibility of proving that the Iraqi regime was linked to Al Qaeda. And third, AAI was suspected of producing poisons and other toxins in a chemical facility located in the village of Sargat, which is east of Halabja in the harsh snowcapped mountains along the Iranian border. OVH was intended to secure the Sargat Chemical Facility and deny AAI's ability to continue and grow their capability. AAI had been operating there for two years and had committed ISIS style atrocities against the Kurds in the area.

AAI overtly controlled a massive area along the border to the east of Halabja. They blatantly flew black flags, blocked roads with machine gun positions, and lived freely in the Sargat valley, and south to the village of Biyara. On AAI's flanks, there were the Islamic Movement of Kurdistan (IMK), as well as the Islamic Group of Kurdistan (IGK). All three groups overtly controlled large sections of Iraqi terrain and had been in control of these areas for several years.

Although OVH was epic, and a spectacular act of textbook Unconventional Warfare (using surrogate or indigenous forces to conduct operations to overthrow governments and/or extremist groups), historically speaking, I am not completely sure that it should be considered a strategic success. We killed a lot of them, but twice as many escaped. Iraq plunged into chaos not long afterwards... AQI emerged, then ISIS. Did we merely scatter them? What if we hadn't driven AAI out and rather opted for some kind of containment and slow eradication strategy instead of a sudden mass-attack? Food for thought as you read my story and do further research.

A note on perspective and artistic choices. I wrote this book intentionally from my singular viewpoint. I didn't use the word "we" very much, and I intentionally did not develop any other characters (my teammates) as an artistic choice. I am not just a self-centered jackass, I simply wanted readers to experience *my* single viewpoint. I also included the story of what we did on the "Green Line" after OVH, because there are a few instances of connectivity to OVH in that part of my story. Also, I reveal a lot of personal moments of disappointment in myself, fear, and weaknesses. I did not write this to make myself look like a hero – I wasn't a hero as you'll see. Also, just because I question the missions I was involved in, this does not mean that I am not proud of my service: I am a patriot.

If you are interested in my evolution from Green Beret to Computer Scientist, or my experiences in the Balkans (including some very unique experiences patrolling alongside the Russian Spetznaz in Kosovo) then read my other book called "One Green Beret," which also includes all of what is in this book.

Follow me on Quora and connect with me on linkedIN for direct questions or comments. The content in this book has been through prepublication review.

Chapter 1
Advanced Force Operations (AFO)
Northern Iraq, PUK Sector, 2003

I walked out of the house with my green duffel bag on my shoulder and shut the door behind me. I could still barely hear my newborn daughter's muffled crying from outside. I stood under my simple house's small covered porch in civilian clothes and took a deep breath of the cold Colorado air. I clenched my eyes and fists and tried to block out the crying and focus: I was on my way to war. I vaguely recognized that five seconds before might have been the last time I would ever see my wife and newborn daughter. I shrugged it all off and drove onto Ft. Carson, ultimately on my way to Iraq.

My team was chosen to perform Advanced Force Operations (AFO); a special type of mission that precedes Unconventional Warfare (UW) and pours the foundation for its success. UW is when Green Berets infiltrate denied areas to rally resistance forces and overthrow governments or terrorist groups. The goal of our AFO mission was to infiltrate Iraq undetected, link up with Kurdish resistance and the CIA, discover the Kurdish resistance forces' composition and disposition, and prepare to receive and integrate the rest of our Special Forces units into the war. There were also two other critical tasks. One was to register "shock and awe" targets against Ansar Al Islam (AAI) and the Iraqi military units along the "Green Line." The other was to repair the airstrip west of As Sulaymaniya, so our brethren would have a place to land. These missions were highly critical to the overarching war strategy. I was about to become part of Task Force Viking, which would later become somewhat legendary within CIA and Special Forces circles.

Soon enough, my team and I landed at an Airbase in Turkey. We had travel orders that legitimized our arrival and purported that we were there for some uneventful training. Soon after landing, we met some mysterious folks from the CIA Special Activities Division, and they told us minimally what we needed to know and do to get ready for our infiltration. We stayed in guest housing as if we were on some routine visit.

The second day we were there, my company commander -a highly intelligent and soft-spoken man- along with some others from the "B-Team," arrived at the guest housing with a line of rental vehicles of random types and colors. They had rented the vehicles as part of applying for a "day pass" at the Air Force base, and they took whatever the rental company had I guess. Of course, we had no intention of ever returning the vehicles to the rental car company since we were going to drive them into Iraq; these rental cars were our official infiltration platform, and we laughed about the day pass.

I was assigned a Jeep Cherokee, and my team also had a red low rider pickup with tinted windows. We all thought the low rider truck was hilarious, and of course we all jokingly wished it had been equipped with hydraulic shocks, so we could optionally bounce into Iraq. The vehicles smelled like cigarettes and had a stuffy feel to them.

I spent most of that day preparing my gear; I loaded magazines, packed ammo, secured hand grenades, and figured out how to hide our guns in the rental vehicles. We waited until dark to load the vehicles so no one else in the guest housing would be able to see us pack our weapons and ammunition under the seats and load our other baggage into the various vehicles. We packed so that we'd be able to pass a shallow cursory check if we were inspected at the border. I was under the impression that if we were to get arrested or detained while trying to cross the border then we would have to fend for ourselves.

The next morning my heart raced anxiously as I got into the driver's seat of my vehicle, which was loaded with hidden weapons and equipment. It was cold, cloudy, and drizzling. I was wearing civilian clothes and a concealed pistol under my jacket. I felt like I was standing at the start point to a marathon or something; my anxiety was tinged with a bit of fear as I pondered all the things that might go wrong at the border, and all the consequences of those things.

I started the Jeep and drove among the small convoy of wacky, weapon laden rental vehicles boldly towards the Airbase's gate, beyond which lied an infinity of unknowns. We showed our day pass to the guards at the Airbase's gate, and we chuckled as they waved us through with bored looks on their faces; they had no idea.

We drove primarily across the southern part of Turkey towards Iraq in what would soon be considered missing rental cars. I began to fully realize the magnitude of my situation; I had just embarked on a low visibility infiltration into a denied country to spearhead an operation that would organize resistance forces, overthrow a government, knock out a major terrorist cell, and bring in hundreds of Green Berets to start a war. I had finally made it to the mission of my dreams.

We were told to be at Habur gate, a border gate that separates Turkey from Iraq, during a very specific time window. I didn't even know where we were supposed to go after we crossed into Iraq, how long it would take to get anywhere, or any other details.

After about an hour of tenuous driving, my nerve endings blasted my body with a tingling sensation in fear as a Turkish police car approached rapidly from behind with its lights flashing. To my relief the police car passed us and then turned in front of our small convoy. I became nervous again when the police car *stayed* in front of us, blue lights still on, and I wondered if someone had somehow organized an escort.

I should have been a lot more scared. We looked like a team of burly professional athletes, all male between the ages of 25 to 35, almost all of us could bench press over 250 pounds and run a half marathon at a moment's notice, and we wore the style of clothes that are typically worn by military men that are off duty. Not to mention, if anyone inspected our vehicles, they would have found an arsenal. I thought that if the Turkish policeman at the border discovered us then we would end up in Turkish prison. If we were caught on the border on the Iraqi side, I just *hoped* that it was all Kurds and that whoever we encountered would be "friendly." I have heard the saying "Hope is not a strategy" before, but in this case, hope was *our only strategy* as we inched our way towards the Iraqi border.

The drive through Turkey was long and dreary due to the weather; I didn't see anything other than razor wire and minefield signs along the Syrian border until we reached far enough east. After a while the foothills of the large mountains along the Iraq border materialized in the distance. We stopped to refuel twice.

During one stop at a tiny run-down gas station, a crowd of about ten or so skinny and dirty men with dark hair formed around me. Most of the men crouched while they smoked cigarettes, and they watched us like we were creatures from another world. One man approached me slowly, and he intently examined my face from less than a foot away, as if he was trying to figure out if I was real or not; I could smell his pungent body odor. I smiled, said hi, and patted him on the shoulder to put the man at ease; he flashed me a mostly toothless grin and walked away a bit embarrassed. I was careful not to make it apparent that I was armed because I didn't know how the Turkish police officer, who had stopped at the gas station with us, would act if he saw a weapon on one of us. I didn't know if he knew who we really were. It was still raining, at times sleeting, and extremely cold.

As I drove along and perceived the scenery before me, I realized that Eastern Turkey is a very rough place. On the last gas stop we made, I saw an entire hillside that looked like a massive pile of mud with sparse grass and the occasional ledge poking out. There were tiny black cave entrances like pockmarks all over it, some of which had satellite dishes mounted in makeshift fashions outside of them and people were squatting or sitting in the mud in the rain outside of the holes. After some subconscious deliberation, I concluded that the holes were their homes. I waved to them and some of them waved back. As we continued driving east, in my mind I wished them all the best. Eastern Turkey made Kosovo look like a five-star hotel, and Bosnia like the Taj Mahal.

As we neared the border, my captain received a call from our people on the other side of the border via satellite phone; they had been there for several months. We were on track for arrival, and apparently they had given my Captain some specific instructions that filtered down to me as "just keep driving when you get there," so I just kept driving the Jeep Cherokee forward. I felt intense anxiety growing in the pit of my stomach. It felt like that day I rode the turret into the center of the UCPMB base camp in Kosovo, except this time it was me who was driving, and the magnitude of this situation was much greater.

Once we were close to the border, and many slow hours had passed, we turned a corner through a large mud puddle in the road and suddenly I saw five or six camera crews filming us drive by! My mind raced and nerves perked, and a flurry of questions streamed through my mind: Who was filming us and why? Had we been caught? Was our whole mission compromised? How did they know we were coming? Will we end up in Turkish prison? Who did they think they were filming? Do they know we are a US Special Forces team? How do I escape? Should we kill them? I quickly realized that I had no choice but to just keep driving and keep hoping, so that's what I did. My anxiety diminished, but only slightly, as I distanced myself from the scene but got closer to the border.

The sun went down, and it was still raining as we approached the lights of Habur gate; the entrance to Iraq. As we neared the border, I thought of the infiltration phase of "Robin Sage" (the epic Green Beret training exercise) and compared it to what I was going though. Instead of being in the back of a truck with a tarp thrown over me in the hills of North Carolina, I was in a rental car approaching Iraq, and I was wearing a North Face jacket and pants with a concealed pistol instead of an Army uniform.

For no particular reason, my expectation was that Habur gate would be similar to that small makeshift gate the UCPMB had constructed in Kosovo. However, the image of that rickety wooden gate in Velja Glava was obliterated as I peered through the foggy windshield at what looked like the lights from a sprawling built-up area. Scattered ambient light from a multitude of windows and street lights emulated from the central area of the gate and made the whole dark and muddled scene before me glow as we approached in the misty darkness.

As we crept towards the inner part of the gate, the stress increased, my heart was pounding super hard, and I had no idea what was going to happen. We were all completely silent as I drove the car slowly and relentlessly forward...painstakingly *forward.* I felt like I had succumbed to the gravitational pull of a black hole. The border was a great analogy for the *event horizon,* because I was either going to die or cross over, and once we crossed there was no turning back. I had one hand on the steering wheel, and I put my locked-and-loaded pistol under my left thigh, so it was accessible from between my legs, but still hidden.

I definitively decided that *I was not going to Turkish prison under any circumstances.* I was prepared to fight my way into Iraq or die trying. I decided that there was no other option.

The tension in my body steadily increased as we approached the final place where I thought we would actually cross the international border into Iraq. It was very dark and my vision was annoyingly blurry. The brake lights on the vehicle in front of me came on, and then the rough image of a Turkish soldier or policeman, I couldn't tell which, materialized in the murky darkness, rain, and dim light. He had oppressively low hanging clouds behind him that reflected eerie grey light downwards from the expansive dark sky. He signaled repetitively for me to continue, like a cop at a traffic circle. I slipped into a robotic state; there was nothing I could do but drive forward until

I was told to stop, and if the Turks tried to stop us then it was go-time. The Turkish cop was on the driver's side of the car when I drove the vehicle past him, and I got the impression from his gestures and the look of strain on his face that he was scared. I wondered frantically if he was directing us to a holding area where our vehicle would be inspected, in which case we'd have been instantly compromised, and my stress and heart rate accelerated even more at the thought as I prepared to react.

We passed the guard, and then suddenly stopped in a narrow area under a bit of overhead cover behind the rest of the convoy. I pondered what had just happened with the Turkish official who just waved us through: Did he know what we were doing there, and who we were, but the Turks were ok with it? Why was that police car driving with most of the time? I quickly realized that I didn't have any answers to questions like this by design. I wasn't supposed to know, none of my assumptions could be confirmed nor questions answered, so I settled on the reality that I didn't need to know any of this anyway. I only needed to listen to my leadership; I trusted them with my life without question. My Captain said to drive forward. That's what I did. [1]

Several of us got out of the car and used a bathroom in an exotically decorated building. The toilets were Middle Eastern hole in the floor style, and there were bright colors, intricate turnings, and stenciling everywhere in the building I went into. Everything seemed very poorly lit, as if there was a veil of darkness and obscurity over everything around me.

As soon as I returned from the bathroom, I got back in the driver's seat and continued onward. Within a few minutes we left the confines of the Habur gate area, and the road started to open up a bit. Through the rain and darkness, my headlights barely provided me the ability to perceive some rather stubby trees along the sides of the road. My Captain told us over the radio that we had officially entered Iraq, and we were headed towards our first linkup with members of a CIA "Ground Branch" team, our unit's "pilot team," and some Kurdish KDP members. The "ground branch" CIA team was a CIA Special Activities Division team, and a Pilot team is a Green Beret team that focuses on preparatory activities related to UW. In my foggy rear-view mirror, I saw the lights of Habur gate fade in the distance through the mist and rain, and we continued deeper into Iraq.

After a few more minutes, we all stopped again along the side of a narrow road lined with small trees, some Kurds got out of vehicles along with some CIA folks, and they all went to my Captain's vehicle. These Kurds were part of the KDP, and they were the first Kurds I had ever seen in my life. The rays of light from my headlights fought the oppressive rain and darkness just sufficiently enough that I could see they were surprisingly clean-cut; thin forms in camouflage uniforms with short dark hair and prominent noses, some wore military style hats. The Kurds told us that the Iraqi Military knew we had arrived, and therefore we needed to travel outside the range of Iraqi "Green Line" artillery and rockets. They told us to follow them the way they suggested, which was to traverse the foothills of the immense mountains along the Turkish border towards our unknown final destination, which was somewhere near As Sulaymaniyah. We had already driven almost all the way across Turkey, but we still had a very long way to go – all the way across Northern Iraq.

The Kurds went back to their vehicles and so did my Captain. I depressed the accelerator again and we continued moving forward. We followed the Kurds along rough winding roads until it was evident even in the pitch blackness that we had climbed up into the mountains. My ears popped several times, and over the course of a few hours the rain turned to sleet, the sleet turned to snow, and as we climbed even higher it was snowing sideways. Huge snowflakes sparkled in my headlights as I struggled to look through the foggy windshield, and for a long time we were in complete whiteout conditions. We were at the complete mercy of the Kurds who were escorting us and had really no choice but to trust them.

I didn't even know where we were *generally* located at any point in time because our GPS was not working. We were moving so slowly through the snowy mountains that periodically Kurds *walked past* my vehicle as it inched along in the whiteout. A few times, the Kurds stood at key places along the roads or trails in order to make sure no one drove off the road and perhaps off a massive cliff. At some point, Kurdish men actually led our ragbag convoy of random rental cars on foot because the visibility was so bad due to the snow.

I drove precariously in this fashion almost all night long, through relentlessly winding and brutal mountain roads and trails. Keeping the windows defogged was nearly impossible, and my vision continued to frustrate me. Nothing at all was visible outside of the cones of light from my headlights, and the cones of light were almost completely full of sparkling white snowflakes. We refueled from containers that the Kurds had in their trucks, which were up near the front of the small convoy.

I was falling asleep at the wheel when we finally broke out of the mountains and it stopped snowing. After a few hours we pulled into a "safe house" somewhere north of Irbil or Mosul somewhere. I got out of the vehicle, and looked around. It was a tremendously austere site, surrounded by those stubby trees. Some KDP personnel shuffled us to a rectangular white concrete block building. They spoke Kurdish to each other, so I didn't understand them. Their mannerisms were welcoming, generous, and polite. The simple building had one room and no heat, and just a thin carpet on a rough poured concrete floor. There was a musty smell in the air inside the room and we all piled in.

It had been 27 hours since we left the Air Force base in Turkey on our 24 hour day pass. I spoke to some of the CIA guys and the Pilot Team very briefly, but it was obvious they were not supposed to tell us very much, or we were all just too tired to talk. Even though I was exhausted from the drive and the stress, it was impossible to get any quality sleep. I just laid there in silence. I couldn't believe I was actually in Iraq, and I had no idea where I was. As I laid there, I thought about my newborn baby daughter, the horrible situation I had left my wife with, and the memories of my amazing grandma who had just died shortly before I left. I also thought about my recent demotion, and how little that and all the associated drama from Kyrgyzstan mattered now that I was finally living my dream war.

The plan for the next morning (only a few hours later since it was already morning) was to drive to a place referred to as "painted rock," which was on the notional border that separated the PUK and KDP portions of Iraqi Kurdistan. I knew the PUK and KDP did not get along, so I could only hope this linkup would go well. There were tribal, political, and many other historical reasons why there was so much tension between the

KDP and PUK, but I just had to survive the linkup at painted rock and continue our mission with the PUK.[2]

I thanked the KDP members, and we loaded into our vehicles again. We took off and followed the KDP and CIA guys in a generally south-easterly direction towards As Sulaymaniyah.

Along the way, there were very few trees anywhere, and the mostly green landscape was massive in scale. To my front right, green rolling hills with exposed ledge mixed with grass extended until fading out to an endless brown expanse that met the horizon. To the north I perceived an enormity of snowcapped peaks that commanded the same degree of respect as the Rocky Mountains did back in Colorado. The sky was uniquely large and foreboding.

As we neared Painted Rock, I realized that it was literally an area along the road where the rocks and exposed ledge were painted many different colors. These wild colored rocks comprised my first introduction to the PUK, a very colorful culture that I learned to appreciate and respect forever. We stopped the vehicles at a sizable washed out dirt area on the side of the road at painted rock and waited for a while. My captain and the CIA guys stood a few meters away, talking on the satellite phone.

Within an hour of sitting in the cold Jeep, I saw a heterogeneous convoy of vehicles in the distance to the east. The convoy approached along the crude, pot hole covered windy road that squirmed through the grassy hills and ledge. The convoy consisted of SUVs and other cars of many colors, and they were sandwiched between two small Nissan pickup trucks with soviet .50 caliber machine guns mounted on them. The PUK Kurds pulled up and started getting out of the vehicles, and I instantly took notice at the vast difference between the uniformed appearances of the KDP as opposed to the PUK members. This was the first time I had actually seen any PUK Kurds, the *Peshmerga* so they're called, and they looked exactly like the way I imagined a true guerilla fighting force would look; I liked them instantly.

They all wore extremely baggy and somewhat tapered dark Khaki pants made of heavy material (which we instantly deemed *MC Hammer pants* due to the similarity). They had AK 47s and other weapons that looked like they had been "bedazzled" with shiny buttons. They had checkered black and white head wraps, tennis shoes, and some of them had flowers sewn into the knit covers that encapsulated the ammunition drums on their AKs. Some had fancy pistols tucked into their light tan cloth belts that they wrapped around their waists (which also served at tourniquets for injuries when needed), and they all had big moustaches, big smiles, and a lot of confidence in their powerful eyes.

The KDP and PUK folks shouted to each other in Kurdish in what seemed like very gruff and awkward ways, as if this hand-off was something that they both wanted to get over with as quickly as possible. After their brief exchange, the KDP departed, and we were left with the PUK guys. Two Green Berets who I hadn't seen in months from back in Colorado jumped out of one of the SUVs that had just arrived with the PUK convoy; they were members of my battalion's Pilot Team.

They wore Kurdish clothing with their US weapons and ammo vests on top. The Pilot Team's Team Sergeant looked hilarious: a white guy with a barely-under-control auburn afro, wearing Oakley sunglasses, with an auburn 1970s moustache, in his MC Hammer pants and PUK shirt, and a combat vest and M4 carbine slung across his chest. We all man-hugged, they complimented us on our red tinted window low rider rental truck, laughed at the fact that the cars might now be officially missing back in Turkey, we laughed at their MC Hammer pants, and we got a quick brief about the threats in the area. It was no more than two or three minutes before we piled back into the vehicles.

The Pilot Team told us that we should always travel between PUK machine gun trucks due to the threat from Ansar Al Islam, IGK, IMK, and the PKK terrorist groups, as well as Iranian, Iraqi, and Syrian Intelligence threats operating throughout the PUK area. I was stunned by the amount of threats, and a persistent feeling of tenseness settled in.[3]

We shook some PUK hands, and then hit the road again. We drove for several more hours. Along the way, I looked south across the terrain towards the "Green Line" out of the right side of the vehicle. The Green Line followed a physical ridge in most places, so it looked like someone drew a crooked line across the entire southern horizon, and it made an interesting backdrop to an almost infinite expanse of green and rocky terrain we were driving through. In some areas along the Green Line, I saw bunkers and radio towers and other indications of Iraqi military presence. I definitely felt like I was in "the enemy's" back yard, because the Green Line was where *two thirds of the Iraqi Army* were positioned as a "front line" facing north against Iraqi Kurdistan, a foreboding site to me as one of a handful of Green Berets who were on their own with no support in a completely unknown place. Looking at the Green Line and all those enemy

Iraqi troops gave me the chills. The endless Iraqi military positions made me feel like an underdog as we drove for several more hours.

When we finally approached the outskirts of As Sulaymaniyah it was so dark I could only perceive it as a cluster of sprawling lights in the distance, which made it look like a giant hovering spacecraft due to the sheer blackness of the backdrop. We took a bypass road around the west side of As Sulaymaniyah that led north towards a village called Qual A Challan, which I soon learned was our final destination.

As we passed As Sulaymaniyah It dawned on me again that we had absolutely no external support from anyone whatsoever; no medical evacuation possible, no air support, no ex-filtration, nothing. So, if we were injured or killed by one of the terrorist groups in the area, or if the Kurds turned on us, or the Iraqis attacked the Kurds (all these situations were considered relatively possible), we were on our own. We had an "evasion plan," but realistically if anything other than a catastrophic loss of rapport with the Kurds happened, we were going to stay and fight to the death alongside the PUK. If the PUK turned on us, and we survived for longer than an instant (unlikely), we would have to escape and evade using any means necessary. They explained to me in Green Beret training that we must be willing to accept conditions such as these, so I didn't put much thought into it.

Finally, we arrived near Qual A Challan where the CIA and the Pilot Team (which acted as a single unit) lived in a cluster of houses. They helped us settle into a different house. Our house had very expensive tile floors, tall ceilings, and it was surrounded by a high brick fence. I cordially greeted a few of the Peshmerga who were outside guarding us and thanked them for doing so. We unloaded the vehicles and organized our equipment and started to talk about how we were going to operate in sectors.

The CIA Branch Chief gave us a warm welcome; he called himself Uncle Andy. He was a retired marine turned CIA operative, and we met the rest of his team. Most of them were former special operators of some kind. Uncle Andy gave us a very thorough briefing about the situation in our area of responsibility, and I was amazed by the area's complexity. The CIA people that briefed us were surprised that my team had not been given *any* of the intelligence they had reported prior to our infiltration. It would have taken weeks to fully comprehend and digest the richness and nuance of the information they had collected. It was a shame that no one ever really saw that information. [4]

After Uncle Andy's overview, we then met several of the key Kurdish leaders, including Bafel Talibani. Bafel was the son of Jalal Talibani – the leader of the PUK, and future president of Iraq. I acquired a genuine PUK uniform, complete with MC Hammer pants, head wrap, and a button-down shirt with "P.U.K." embroidered on it. We wore these until the war started, so when we drove around we blended in better (at least from a distance). There was a satellite TV in our house, so we watched the news to see how the situation was developing. One day I watched someone on the news deny that the US had anyone in Iraq yet.

After we decided our sectors, I was in charge of figuring out where we should integrate our Alpha Company into the Kurdish units once they arrived (whenever the war actually started). My sector spanned the territory between As

Sulaymaniya all the way up to Taq Taq and then north along the boundary between the PUK and KDP, all the way to Turkey and Iran. Taq Taq was almost on the Green Line, and at the western most edge of the PUK area.

My sector was an enormous area, I would guess around 5000 square kilometers. I remember standing about 6 feet away from the giant map we had taped to the wall, and my area looked like an imperceptible mass. Some of the areas of my sector took five or six hours to reach by vehicle from Qual A Challan. I really didn't know where to begin, and I had to figure out where 6 Teams would live and operate when they arrived, and I didn't have a lot of time. The other guys on my team formed sub teams and had other sectors with responsibility to bring in our B and C companies.

The most important sector for sure was not mine, it was the area east of Halabja where the Ansar Al Islam (AAI) radical Islamic group controlled a very large and brutally mountainous area against the Iranian border. The Islamic Group of Kurdistan (IGK), and the Islamic Movement of Kurdistan (IMK) groups also operated there, and both of their territories were connected to the north and south borders of the AAI enclave, respectively. During random conversations with the Peshmerga about AAI (the Kurds are Muslim) over tea, I learned that *radical* Islam is not Islam at all; radical "islamists" are just gangs of psychos that generate ridiculous interpretations of religion to use as excuses for their behavior. AAI had a poison and chemical production facility in a small village called Sargat, which is near a village called Khurmal. These were two very important places for us.

Once the CIA and Pilot team provided my team a sufficient level of situational awareness, we started working our sectors as best we could. I drove, with two Peshmerga machine gun trucks for security and my SUV in the middle, out to my sector almost every day with the goal of collecting details about the disparate Peshmerga units, and trying to find the best places for our brethren teams to stay when they arrived. It was difficult to know where to go; the maps we had did not reflect the nuances of reality at all. The Peshmerga gave us tips of where to go and helped us get there. Without them we would have been ineffective, and we wouldn't have been safe traveling around. It was also difficult simply because of the distances we had to drive to find various PUK groups. Some days I drove for 8 or 10 hours, just to meet a single group of Peshmerga in a village somewhere for an hour or so to see what was there. Often when we arrived at various places (dozens of places) we were disappointed to discover that there weren't many fighters there, or they lacked weapons, or the village wouldn't have been suitable for one of our teams to operate from. We also only had one real interpreter, so as a team we couldn't easily explore the whole PUK area simultaneously.

Managing all the data we collected on our computers, and digitally transmitting that data back to our headquarters was very challenging. None of us were technology professionals, so managing large amounts of photos that linked to documents was frustrating and error prone. Also, the technology at the time was not as capable as it is today. Moreover, we were using a certain type of radio that made it difficult to transmit large files, like photos. We tried to transmit every couple of days, and sometimes it took dozens of attempts and many hours to get the information back. The information that *did* make it back was difficult for the guys on the other end to piece together because we had to break all the files into pieces, and then send the pieces over different transmissions. Therefore, hyperlinks didn't work, document and photos were hard to put into context, and ultimately the information we sent was very hard for the recipients to consume.

Due to these challenges, we were afraid we wouldn't get our job done before the war kicked off. It was nerve-racking to say the least. It was also at times frustrating because I had unrealistic expectations for what the Kurds would tell us.

On one occasion, during one of the long trips into my sector, my colleague and I encountered a band of PUK fighters that numbered in the hundreds. For each element of Peshmerga that we discovered, we always asked them a few standard questions about their capabilities and disposition. We needed to know what the Kurds would do if the Iraqis invaded Kurdistan, and in the event that such an invasion happened, we needed to know which areas would be protected by which Kurdish groups. This one experience, near the village of Taq Taq, was a good lesson in the simplicity and effectiveness of the PUK Peshmerga groups.

As I approached this PUK unit's compound, at the end of a muddy dirt road in a hilly area, a large group of armed Peshmerga with thick mustaches, MC Hammer pants, and black and white checkered head wraps started to materialize and become clearer through the light fog. They gathered around our vehicle as I depressed the brakes, and I heard them murmuring curiously in Kurdish. I opened the door and stepped out slowly. Since I was wearing a PUK uniform but I obviously wasn't Kurdish, they looked at me cautiously. I waved and smiled to make sure they realized I was friendly, and I asked if I could speak to the leader of their group. A man raised his hand and stepped forward, he was 5 foot 8 or so, probably in his 50s. He had very intelligent and intense eyes, wore the classic Kurdish pants as well as a combat vest full of AK magazines, and his AK was slung on his shoulder. We shook hands and exchanged greetings, and I walked a few meters with him into a block building and we sat down on the thin carpet that covered the concrete floor. A younger Kurd brought us tea and I thanked him respectfully. I asked the leader of this group, like I had many other leaders of many other small groups in the previous weeks, via our interpreter, a series of questions that amounted to a dialog something like this:

"If the Iraqis attack, then what areas would your group protect and operate in?"

"We will *attack* them wherever they are" he answered calmly, but he stirred and seemed a bit confused by this question and tried to be respectful with his answer, then I countered again.

"Well if you attack them *there* and they flank you, who will attack the flanking Iraqi element?"

He stirred a bit more, and his eyes narrowed a bit

"...We will just attack them on the flank as well...and anywhere else they are...and if we need more Peshmerga, then inshallah they will come."

After making some small talk with this Peshmerga leader for a few minutes, we were done, and I went back outside. I shook a few hands on the way to our vehicle, and within a few minutes we were on our way back to Qual A Challan. This encounter taught me that the Peshmerga did not really embrace defense as a strategy. The Peshmerga specialize in *offense*, even as a means of defense. The US military thinks very mechanically about combat operations and tactics, and my expectation was to hear similar mechanics from the Peshmerga. This was a senseless expectation to have, and I would see very soon how effective the Kurds were in real combat.

After many instances of conversations like the one I just described with various tribes and villages and militia units over the course of the next month or so, I kind of settled into the routine of the mission. We incrementally built a depiction of where the PUK had fighters, where those fighters could and would operate, and what kind of weapons they had or could acquire. We continued to find which areas were most suitable to become the places where the incoming Green Beret teams would live once they arrived and the war started. The incoming teams needed to be located in areas of tactical significance, where they could best assist the most Kurdish units and have the best access to infrastructure such as electricity, and water, and roads, and places to buy basic necessities. So, we spent the next month doing an "Unconventional Warfare Assessment" in which the goal was to depict where all the Kurds were, and find a suitable home for each of our incoming teams. I had paper notes stuck all over that big paper wall map.

Repairing the As Sulaymaniya West Airstrip so that it was operational again was one of the most important tasks of our AFO mission. We had infiltrated Iraq with an Air Force Special Tactics Squadron (STS) guy, along with about $320,000.00 cash in order to pay Kurdish construction workers to fix the runway. The STS guy was there as an operator on our team, to certify the runway, and direct aircraft once the war started. We needed to fix the runway so MC-130s could bring the rest of our Green Beret brothers into the fight when the war officially started.

Soon my team leadership decided that we might fail our mission if we stayed in Qual A Challan; it just took too long to get anywhere from there, we were short on interpreters, and the prolonged exposure on the roads was too risky because the Kurds had information that AAI planned to attack us via vehicular suicide bombings and drive-by tactics. So, we planned to move to the Peshmerga Headquarters that was a few miles west of the As Sulaymaniyah Airstrip to decrease travel time and risks, and to be closer to the work being done on the Airstrip.

A few days later we moved down to the Kurdish Headquarters near As Sulaymaniyah West (ASW). Since we basically "lived off the land" in the modern sense of the phrase, it was very easy to move from place to place. It was here at ASW that we became even more integrated into the daily life of the Peshmerga. We got to know key Kurdish leaders, and they took great care of us. I was reminded of my times in Bosnia, living among the local people and realizing how amazing they are. The PUK built us showers, and they even acquired "regular" toilets for us, even though they really didn't understand what we thought was so great about them. We met soldiers' families, and got to know and love the Kurdish culture. I spoke German to one of the commanders all the time, his eye had been shot out by AAI a few months prior near Halabja. He was like my personal interpreter at times, and we liked to talk about the differences between what I saw in Kurdistan vice what it was like in America. The minister of defense equivalent to the PUK also spoke German, so my Captain and I were able to communicate well with him. Both my Captain and I were quite proficient in German, we had "fluency" according to the Defense Language Proficiency Test (DLPT). Since it's common for Kurds to perform migrant work in Germany many of them spoke German. This allowed us to talk to quite a few people without an interpreter, which was very handy. It was especially useful when the Minister of defense and other Kurdish leaders wanted to speak to us in private sometimes.

We almost always ate dinner with them. They put all the food in big trays on a high table, and everyone just stood around the table and dug into the trays to fill their plate, usually with large spoons. The women never ate with us, but there always seemed to be a few of them peeking out from the kitchen area, probably just wanting to see what an American looked like. I adapted and grew quite fond of Kurdish life; the fried grass, the outstanding tea, the baklava, and the unbelievable strength and kindness. The fried grass was a bit prickly, but we got used to it, and it became a favorite of mine. The tea was usually red, and the Kurds served it in small vase-like glass cups that were about three or four inches high and an inch in diameter. They put very raw sugar in the bottom of each glass, and I would stir in as much as I wanted as they filled and refilled the elegant little cups.

There were hundreds, possibly thousands of Peshmerga in ASW, and it was only a twenty-minute drive to the airfield and an hour to get into my sector. We were able to cover way more of our area of responsibility at a much faster pace. Our productivity increased by the day, and so did our rapport with the Peshmerga.

One day, four IMK members attacked ASW; the PUK killed them all before they even got past the gate. When I heard the gunfire just a few hundred meters away I became hyper aware of our situation. This incident made it official that these extremist groups knew we were there, and they wanted us dead. The PUK told us there were bounties on our heads, and that there had even been pictures of us distributed somehow, kind of like "Wanted" posters from the Wild West.

As the threat of IMK, IGK, and AAI increased in the area, we began to treat our Air Force guy like a VIP; if he was killed, who would validate the runway, and how would the rest of our unit get there if the runway was untrustworthy? I was put in charge of working with the Kurdish security folks to make sure they had what they needed to implement the right security controls at ASW.

One day out of nowhere we were told via our satellite phone, that four Iraqi MIG fighter jets had just taken off from near Baghdad and they were headed north. I translated "headed north" into "coming to kill us." I immediately assumed they were headed towards our location on a bombing run to take us out as a preemptive strike. One of the Iraqi's potential courses of action was to launch a "hail Mary" attack into Northern Iraq against the Kurds; possibly a *chemical* attack. We immediately informed the Kurds, we all ran away from the building and spread out as much as possible, and we made sure we had our gas masks. While I was lying in the grass a few hundred meters from the building, nerves throbbing and heart slapping my t-shirt, anxiously and fearfully listening for the sound of incoming jets, I wondered what they would tell my wife if I died at that moment. Luckily, the jets never arrived, but this was another stark reminder of how isolated we were. [5], [6]

Before long I had collected and reported all the info I could for my sector, and we as a team had sufficiently finished figuring out where all the Kurds *were*. I had walked through minefields with Kurds to get better vantage points on the Iraqis to collect grid coordinates of critical Iraqi positions. I saw large piles of human feces in remote sites along the green line because there were no facilities, but hundreds of Kurds were staged there. I saw PKK positions in the distance along the Turkish border. I saw a red haired Kurd blow bubbles into his motorcycle gas tank with a large straw to mix the fuel and then take off for the Green Line to collect information for us. I was denied a hand shake and told to leave one village because the US had left the Kurds hanging back in the 90s. I saw an infinite amount of amazing courage and cunning in the Kurds while deciphering their composition and disposition (with extensive help from my leadership). Finally, in mid-March 2003, we finalized the As Sulaymaniyah airstrip and our Air Force guy gave it his official blessing, and we knew where we were going to place all the incoming teams.

It was the second half of March and we still didn't know when the rest of the Green Berets in my unit would arrive, nor when the war would actually start. Turkey still wouldn't let anyone in, and I was feeling very stranded and isolated; one of a handful of Green berets and CIA guys, embedded with the Peshmerga for over two months. We went to Jalal Talabani's (the future president of Iraq and leader of the PUK) house near the Dukan dam and briefed him on our plans. I wasn't personally involved in the meeting, but according to my Captain, "Mam Jalal" thought we were doing ok.

While we waited for "higher" to tell us when the war was going to start, we shifted our focus to targeting AAI. We made many trips into Halabja, which was very near where AAI operated. Halabja was on the outskirts of the brownish green foothills of the massive snowcapped peaks along the Iranian border. Every time we approached the area, AAI spotted our small groups of SUVs, and they launched rocket and mortar attacks against us and the Peshmerga headquarters. On one such occasion, a Kurd was killed by the tailfin of a katoosha rocket that had screamed in and exploded several yards away. This was the first time I had heard the sound of incoming mortars and rockets...they don't whistle...they sound more like the whoosh of a small airplane, but faster.

We performed repetitive reconnaissance operations on the border of AAI's territory to register targets for the shock and awe campaign. I spent a lot of time sitting behind a high powered spotting scope with a CIA guy on the edge of AAI's territory. He wrote down coordinates as I plotted with a laser range finder. We registered anything we saw that looked like it might be a defensive position or a place where AAI fighters might consolidate.

At one point, the PUK made some kind of deal (that I was unaware of) with the IGK that permitted us to enter into IGK territory to get a better look at AAI, because inside IGK territory we would have several great vantage points on AAI. Once the arrangement was solidified, three of us, along with one CIA guy, drove nervously through IGK's dusty entrance gate. I was incredibly tense as we passed several heavy machine gun positions that were manned by bearded, dirty fighters who wore ragged tan combat gear as well as wide black headbands with white Arabic writing on them. My nervousness spiked as the men glared at us with an unsettling, calm intensity. IGK had no idea that we were not only there to register shock and awe targets against AAI, but we were *also* there to register shock and awe targets against *them*. I captured waypoints on my GPS as we drove past more machine gun positions, and others took notes on azimuths and distances from the waypoints so we could later produce coordinates of key positions. We were deep inside IGK territory for several hours, registered several key AAI targets from relatively concealed locations, and then drove back out the same way we came in.

As part of our shock and awe targeting efforts against AAI, I spent one night in a snowstorm on a hilltop, next to a dead Kurd, receiving sporadic mortar fire from AAI, with no overhead protection, in a wet sleeping bag.

We also continued to register Iraqi military locations along the Green Line for the shock and awe. On one occasion, we did a classic recon operation to identify key Iraqi positions along the Green Line. We geared up, had our rucksacks filled, and set out to occupy a ridgeline north of a village called Cham Chamal, which was very close to the Green Line. After our arrival, we set out on foot along a very large ridge as if we were sneaking around to avoid detection. However, we soon realized there were PUK guys everywhere, and they started asking us why we were carrying so much stuff. I guess they were curious as to where we could possibly be going that we would need so much. We quickly realized that even though we were only about a kilometer from the Iraqis, they could not distinguish us from the Kurds. The final tip that made me realize we were being silly was when a couple Kurds showed up with a platter of meats and a pot of tea. I quickly realized, greatly humbled, that we didn't need to recon anything; the Kurds already knew where all the Iraqi positions were, and what was at each one. They drew information onto the maps that we carried, and pointed out into the distance, describing in unbelievable detail what was along the Green Line, and *behind* the Green Line, which we were now casually observing from the ridgeline north of Cham Chamal as we sipped tea and ate meat off of a platter. I learned a lesson: The Kurds were smarter than us, and we learned to accept that fact and leverage it. We were not experts in war, *they were*, in fact I felt like an idiot when it came to war compared to the Peshmerga. The Peshmerga are a culture of warriors that spans generations, a fighting force like no other.

I began to wonder if the war would ever start, and if the rest of my unit would ever arrive. However, in late March, apparently someone up the chain decided that it was time to use another option to get the rest of the Green Berets into Northern Iraq immediately; I guess the only option was to fly over enemy territory. I was notified at the last minute, when the aircraft were already on their way.

These daring flights, which carried two battalions of Green Berets over hostile territory, eventually became known as "The Ugly Baby." They flew the entire 2nd and 3rd Battalions of the 10th Special Forces group on the longest MC130 Talon combat flight in history; all the way from Jordan, over Iraq, and into Northern Iraq over significant anti-aircraft fire.

Some of my team stayed in Halabja, but I scrambled to get my gear together, and then I headed for the As Sulaymaniyah airstrip to handle the reception of our teams. Within a few hours, I stood on the edge of the ASW runway looking into the dark sky, and I overheard the intense fear-laden radio traffic from the pilots as they evaded anti-aircraft fire. We prepared buses to get the teams out to their designated locations so they could link up with their assigned Peshmerga units. Thousands of Kurds constituted a huge perimeter around the airstrip, and we blocked off every road including the main ones. No one was permitted to enter.

We set up lights along the runway so the aircraft would be able to identify it easier, and I listened to the pilots feverishly screaming status over the radio as they flew in the Ugly Baby. It was intense beyond imagination as I listened to their radio chatter. As per Murphy's law, as the Talons prepared for final approach, a Kurd accidentally fired an RPG into the air (it was slung on his shoulder facing up when it went off), and the generator that was running the lights on the runway died, resulting in a completely blacked-out airstrip. For a moment, the pilots questioned the security of the airstrip, and my leadership convinced them it was OK. I was glad that I was already on the ground.

The aircraft were shot to shit. The Air Force STS guy had trouble vectoring the pilots onto the airstrip as they approached, so he employed an ingenious tactic. He jumped in the Jeep Cherokee and sped off down the runway to "lead the plane by the nose;" his plan was to drive the vehicle to the end of the airstrip, with the headlights on, and then drive back down towards where I was in order to give the pilots a reference point as they approached. I was confused as to why this was necessary, as I assumed that the pilots had night vision, but since the Air Force STS guy said it was required, I believed it because when it came to Aircraft, he was the ultimate authority.

I was in charge of security on the ground for the Ugly Baby, and I was constantly talking to guys that we had embedded out on the roadblocks to report the situation from our flanks. There were thousands of cars backed up along every avenue of approach leading to the road that passed the Airstrip. The explosion from the accidental RPG round occurred at a time that we actually thought it might have been the Iraqis launching rockets from the Green Line.

It was an incredible scene: an Air Force guy maniacally driving in front of a wounded MC130 aircraft down a newly repaired airstrip that we could only hope would hold up once the planes touched down on it. An RPG exploded and hundreds of Kurds chattered as they tried to get a look at my night vision goggles and day/night sniper scope on my rifle. I had constant situation reports streaming in to my radio headset because hundreds of cars were now backed up on the roads leading in as people reported to me from the roadblocks, and Ltc Tovo kept asking me what was going on and if everything was secure. Truth be told, I had no idea if anything was truly secure.

Finally, the aircraft screamed in and clattered noisily down the airstrip to where I was standing along with a few hundred Peshmerga. The two aircraft looked so huge and black that they appeared blacker than the darkness that surrounded them, the smell of fuel was alarming, and they were so loud and monstrous the crowd of curious Kurds instantly began to encircle them in awe, as if an alien spacecraft had landed. The plane was smoking from the damage it had incurred from taking fire during its journey over denied air space, and it was dripping fuel, which made us fearful of an explosion. The birds came to a complete stop, and the pilots lowered the tailgates. Dim reddish light spilled out of the tailgate onto the runway, and I perceived human forms run down the ramp and some knelt and kissed the ground. My feeling of isolation faded as I watched dozens of my fellow Green Berets unload. I expected to take rocket fire from the Iraqis, and I was surprised by their lack of response since there were thousands of them only a short distance away along the Green Line, and we were in rocket range.

We had prepared buses to take the teams to the Kurdish villages that we had identified for them. The Kurds and I helped the incoming teams find the right buses to bring them to their respective Peshmerga hosts. I saw people that I hadn't seen in months from other teams and companies back in Colorado. They were surprised to see me because they didn't know we were already in Iraq. We had prepared packets of information for each team, and the packets told them about the place they were going and the Peshmerga leadership they would link up with. I was stunned when one of the guys told me that they hadn't received any of the information we, the CIA, nor the Pilot team had reported the whole time we'd been there on AFO. Information and Intelligence flow had been an abysmal failure; the teams had absolutely no idea where they were going nor who their Kurdish militia leaders were. It was terrible, but like good Green Berets, they were accustomed to operating on little to no information for extended periods of time under extremely tenuous conditions, so they were all smiles, and ready to go wherever they needed to.

As the buses faded from view and the chaos subsided, the crowd of Kurds cleared and Ltc Tovo patted me on the back. I radioed to the roadblocks to let traffic flow again. I let out a massive sigh of relief. It was surreal. We had infiltrated Northern Iraq, linked up with the CIA, discovered where all the Kurds were, figured out where to put our teams, registered tons of shock and awe targets, and successfully infiltrated two battalions of Green Berets into Northern Iraq according to plan; the AFO mission was a success.

The war still hadn't officially started yet, and I left for Halabja to link up with the rest of my team to prepare for the operation that would be the end of my quest for war: the assault on Ansar Al Islam, which would later become known as *Operation*

Viking Hammer; the largest single Unconventional Warfare attack in the History of the Green Berets.

On the way down the road to Halabja in the dark morning hours, in the back seat of an SUV driving behind a Kurdish gun truck, my mind raced thinking about what I was about to encounter.

Chapter 2
From the Ugly Baby to Operation Viking Hammer
Halabja area, Northern Iraq, 2003

Once we arrived at the PUK headquarters in Halabja, I looked around to find the rest of my team. The Headquarters building had been damaged by so much sporadic mortar and rocket fire from AAI over the years that I think they gave up trying to keep windows in it. I quickly found my team in a small grey room, very plain, no windows, with a poured concrete floor. I settled in.

We spent the next day planning with C Company, who was in charge of the attack. My team was the only team from B Company in Halabja, because we were familiar with the area and the Kurdish leadership due to repetitive exposure to the situation during AFO. The general plan was to perform tactical preparations and recons for a few days, then we would mount the assault when my leadership felt like we had sufficiently planned and had some dedicated airpower. The Peshmerga leadership thought we should attack immediately, because we were just giving AAI too much time to prepare for our attack, and an opportunity for key people to escape. The Kurds reluctantly agreed to wait, although waiting was certainly not their style. We were also waiting to find out when the "Shock and Awe" barrage was going to happen. During the AFO mission we registered almost 70 targets against AAI, as well as hundreds of others along the Green Line, and we were wondering when that payload would arrive. Most of this planning took place between the C company commander, my Battalion commander, and each team's leadership. They decided who would comprise the

"Attack Prongs." I thought the officers in charge of this operation were brilliant; they always accounted for things that I never thought of.

Finally, it was Shock and Awe night, which signaled the official start of the Iraq war in 2003. On that night, I stood on the roof of the Kurdish headquarters, with a very clear view of AAI's giant mountain den. The crooked outline of AAI's mountains along the Iranian border was so black it was barely discernable from the night sky. I stood next to my battalion commander, Ltc Tovo.

All the people on the roof became silent, and I heard an ominous buzzing sound materialize from the distant sky behind me. The noise then changed from a buzz to a low hum, like the sound of a very small and slow aircraft, and it was, in slow gradations, increasing in volume and decreasing in range. In only a few seconds, the sounds multiplied, then became omnipresent and louder, and I deduced that they were coming from multiple directions. The eerie sounds grew and surrounded me until I felt like I was standing within some kind of robotic, relentless swarm of bees that were invisible in the night sky as they streamed overhead towards AAI's mountains. I watched AAI's tracers fly straight up in the air and listened to automatic weapons fire as AAI and IGK positions started firing wildly into the sky at the sounds. A Kurdish man behind me giggled at their pathetic attempt to stop the Tomahawk missiles that mindlessly approached their mountain fortress.

The black mountainside was suddenly saturated with oxygen-quivering explosions of fire in rapid succession; it was really an immeasurable and unexplainable level of violence. The explosions looked like the surface of boiling water when it reaches a "rolling boil," except instead of rolling froth on the surface this was continuous orange and red *flames* against an enormous blanket of darkness. I thought I was going to count the explosions, but once the Tomahawks started hitting, there was no way to count them; it was the most relentless and devastating thing I had ever seen in my life. There were at least thirty or forty that all hit within less than a minute; the concussion from each strike became a part of the air I breathed, and I felt each explosion in my gut. Straggler missiles continued to buzz over our heads for the next hour or so and wreaked further havoc. Not only had AAI been bombed, but the IGK positions we registered were also hit.

The next day, the Kurdish PUK commander was not entirely convinced that the tomahawk strikes had been as effective as they were sensational. He thought the AAI fighters probably heard the missiles approaching and had time to get away from anywhere that would have been obviously targeted. However, he did agree that we may have taken out a few of their heavy weapons, such as mortars, and possibly some landmines, which was a positive. I was told that we had killed over 100 IGK members at their headquarters near Khurmal.

We continued preparation for Operation Viking Hammer; planning, mortar attacks, and reconnaissance were the duties for the next couple days.

Myself and a few other "mortar men" (The 18B MOS is highly proficient in mortars) from C company loaded our 81mm mortars into a truck along with a few dozen rounds of ammo, and as many Kurds as we could fit. We drove southeast towards the AAI enclave outside of Biyara to a planned location where we could strike some of the AAI positions with the mortars. We drove until we found a good spot behind the crest of a hill and sent spotters up to the top of the ridge to find some AAI positions. I was a spotter.

As I stayed low on the ridge, I peered across the expansive layers of ridgelines, I noticed that AAI was very well dug into the mountains, and they had established many positions in depth. AAI were not amateurs; they had controlled their 300 square kilometer mountain area for more than two years, and they were prepared to defend it.

Soon we had established a target, and we spotted some actual AAI fighters meandering around it. I watched their bearded forms through a spotting scope, and I guessed that they were licking their wounds from the tomahawk barrage; I saw them talking and I could read their expressions. It was alarming to look at other human beings through the mortar site, thinking that I was about to start killing them, but any one of them would have chopped my head off if they could. Since we didn't see any mortars on their side anywhere close, we decided to bring the mortars up to the top of the ridge so we could use a technique called "direct lay," which is much faster and less technical way to fire mortars. We quickly analyzed the AAI bunker; it had thick overhead cover. This meant that if a mortar exploded on top, it might shake them up a bit, but probably wouldn't kill them. So, we had to get creative.

We developed a plan to drop "sub-surface burst" rounds onto the top of the positions, immediately followed by a volley of "near-surface burst" rounds. Sub-surface burst rounds do not explode when they hit the ground, they explode on a time delay *after* they hit the ground. This means the weight of the plummeting round will drive it into the overhead cover before it explodes, thus penetrating their overhead protection before exploding. This would cause the AAI guys to either die in place or run out of the bunker into the open. The near surface burst rounds explode about 4 meters off the ground and are designed to spray shrapnel downward in a cone, which is very effective against "troops in the open." Our idea was that the sub-surface barrage would force them to evacuate the bunker only to find themselves in a hail of explosions and shrapnel from rounds exploding over their heads. It was ingenious, albeit quite brutal.

I was a gunner on one of the 81MM tubes. By "gunner" I mean I was working the sight, levels, and "dialing in" the mortar instruments to get the rounds, and keep the rounds, on target (mortars are very mechanically sophisticated). We gave the Kurds a quick class on how to safely drop the mortars down the tube, most of them knew how already, and soon I had a young, very excited Kurd ready to drop the first one. I lined up the mortar system perfectly with the target, but I knew that the first couple rounds would settle the baseplate and would significantly move the mortar, so I had to be quick about getting realigned, especially since I expected AAI to return fire.

I told the first Kurd to drop the round, and he did. The tube made a loud "poomf" sound, the baseplate sank into the ground, and I quickly realigned the mortar site and waited for impact. The round landed very close, so I quickly calculated the offset, realigned, and told the next guy to drop the subsequent rounds. I was on target within three rounds and the baseplate was decently settled. I then instructed the Kurds to line up and administer the sequenced barrage.

The Kurds all stared at me with eager expressions on their faces; probably fifteen of them. They looked like a line in a department store, but instead of holding merchandise while waiting to pay, they were holding mortar rounds in the middle of the mountains, and I was the cashier. They walked up and dropped their rounds one by one the way we showed them. I realigned between each round until all the rounds were sent. The first round hit before the line finished. I watched through the mortar site, and the others watched through spotting scopes, as the mortars started to hit in rapid succession; I saw our plan come to life.

Several mortars landed near or on top of the large position (mortars are not pinpoint accurate). Through the dust I saw the AAI fighters try desperately to scramble out of the damaged position, some moved as if they were wounded already. When they reached a few feet away from the cover of the bunker, they were engulfed in overhead explosions. One of them was directly under a near surface burst blast. I saw his body contort, and then crumble lifelessly to the ground into an unnatural shredded heap through the lens of my mortar site.

As I expected, we started receiving AAI mortar fire, and although this was super scary initially, their fire was wildly inaccurate. Their rounds landed several hundred meters to my southeast, and subsequent rounds were all over the place; very inconsistent. The Kurds said the AAI mortars probably have no sights (which they claimed was quite common because it's hard to find working sights on the black market). During the day, we fired dozens of 81 MM mortars, and killed several AAI fighters, wounded others, and damaged a few fortified positions. We picked everything up and headed back to Halabja. From this day on we referred to what happened as "dueling mortars day."

The next day it was my team's turn to conduct reconnaissance operations, which meant we were going to penetrate AAI's territory. One of the guys on my team was an expert with the Barrett .50 Cal sniper rifle (a very large semi-automatic sniper rifle capable of killing at ranges over a mile away). Our plan was to penetrate about two kilometers into AAI territory, set up a position with the Barrett from which we had about a 1000 meter shot at a major AAI position on a hilltop that we referred to as "the pillbox." We thought we may be able to spot some AAI leadership and take them out.

We drove the vehicle slowly down the road, under cover, masked by terrain, until we reached a stopping point on the road about 1500 meters inside AAI's territory. An eerie, primal feeling came over me when we penetrated their territory. The Barrett gunner and I got out and walked across the road and down the steep embankment so we would be partially hidden from view. The terrain had no trees at all, and the ground was littered with fragments of flat stones and patches of grass. I felt overconfident that day, maybe all the air power and mortaring had given me a bit of a superiority complex.

As my gunner got situated behind the Barrett rifle, and I scanned the pillbox with the scope on my M21, suddenly a massive burst of machine gun fire snapped over my head and made powder out of some of the stones around me. The other guys were also taking fire over by the vehicle, and they jumped down behind a small roll of earth on the side of the dirt road.

My heart rate was instantly pegged as my gunner and I slid down just under the crest of the hill to get behind cover. I deduced that the rounds were coming from several heavy machinegun positions. I heard a flurry of noise from the direction of the pillbox that loosely correlated to the snapping sounds above my head. The guys on the road nominated one person to run to the truck to get ready to drive. Through the dust and noise, I watched them all dash for the vehicle. There was no way my gunner and I would have made it that far to the truck because the machine gun fire was all over the road above us. Using my radio, I told our Captain we would take the valley behind me back to the west, and then we would break north and link up with them back where we had some cover. Just as I started hustling down into the valley behind me, thinking I was safe, I heard a horrible tearing sound in the huge sky above. I realized in an instant that it was the sound of an incoming mortar round. I'd heard mortars before, but this one seemed different. The sound got closer and closer, and I knew it was big and it was going to land close to us; my body tightened as if I had turned to stone with fear.

The 120-millimeter mortar slammed into the ground with unimaginable force and detonated no more than 40 meters away from me. I was facing it and saw it explode clearly; it sprayed dirt and rocks up and outwards like when a drop of liquid hits the surface of water, but with spectacular rapidity and violent energy. The concussion from the detonation rippled through my body and I involuntarily fell to my knees while my ears and head rang like a bell. Although my ears rang intensely, I still heard shrapnel and dirt and stone zinging through the dusty air as bullets continued to snap overhead. I yelled to my gunner to see if he was OK as I patted myself frantically looking for indications of shrapnel wounds; neither one of us was hit.

The round had landed just on the other side of a sizable piece of exposed ledge, and that sliver of ledge was between us and the explosion, so I think it deflected the shrapnel away from us. It was pure luck we were not killed or mutilated. We brushed ourselves off and continued to run lower into the gully. I tried to radio to my Captain, but we had lost radio communications with him. We continued to follow the ravine, and soon I was not exactly sure where we were. I thought AAI would dispatch a small contingent of fighters to track us down, but they either didn't, or we evaded them successfully.

I was thankful when I heard the Peshmerga firing mortars to suppress the AAI positions, and some of our guys also fired the MK19 machine gun at their positions. After about 20 lonely minutes in the bottom of a massive valley floor, we were back inside friendly lines, and we linked up with the rest of the team. Our sniper/recon mission turned out to be totally pointless and it had almost cost us our lives. I learned to never get complacent again.[7]

We made our way back to the Halabja headquarters. I felt extensively humbled, shaken up, and downright lucky. I cleaned my rifle, hung out with the Kurds and had some tea, and we told our war story to everyone, much to their entertainment. The Kurds told us we were lucky that AAI didn't capture and publicly behead us.

The next day I stood among all of C Company, watching our leadership and the Peshmerga leaders walk everyone through the final attack plan for Operation Viking Hammer. I could tell that the Kurdish leaders were not enthused about the depth of planning detail we had forced them to think through and explain.[8]

The C Company B-Team had built a gigantic terrain model of the entire AAI enclave. The model was built "to scale" out of dirt, and it was probably 40 feet by 40 feet square. Terrain models are fundamental in military planning, and this was the mother of all terrain models that I had ever seen. The Kurdish leaders, and the leader of each prong, used long sticks as pointers to walk through their piece of the plan. I was proud of the way my captain talked through our piece. The plan, in summary, was quite simple from our perspective. Most of my team was the "main effort" of the attack, and we were called the *yellow prong*. Our responsibility was to secure the chemical facility in Sargat and clear the small village further east called Daramar. The Green prong consisted of the other half of my team and several personnel from C Company, and their mission was to cover our advances up the Sargat valley by clearing the ridge to our north. There were orange and red prongs as well, and they were responsible for zones south of us.

The leader of each prong finished briefing their plans. The PUK leadership and my officers declared that we were ready to go. I was told my battalion commander and Uncle Andy spoke to Donald Rumsfeld on the phone, and he said it was time to go for it.

The preparations for war were over. Now it was time to fight.

Chapter 3
Operation Viking Hammer
Sargat Valley, Northern Iraq, 2003

I laid on the concrete floor on a short piece of foam padding, trying to keep warm. I listened to everyone on my team nervously tossing and turning in the pitch blackness of our grey concrete room at the PUK headquarters in Halabja. My M21 sniper rifle was perched on its bipod next to me; it was the tool that I would carry into battle against a thousand AAI extremists in the morning. I had my hand on its buttstock most of the night, thinking about how after 12 years of service, my big day had finally come. During the night, I left the room and unloaded all my magazines, 20 of them, to make sure the springs were properly stretched so I wouldn't have a feed malfunction during the battle. I actually went through this ritual twice, because I thought I had forgotten to check one of the magazines the first time. I heard my captain leave the room once with all of his combat gear, probably to do some similar preparations.

Finally, at about 4 AM, after a mostly sleepless night, one of our most familiar Peshmerga leaders came in and told us that it was time to go. I ate breakfast silently standing around a rustic table with about a dozen of the Kurdish PUK Peshmerga leaders in a dimly lit room. It was fried eggs and rice. I scanned the faces of the warriors standing around the table in full Peshmerga garb, some of our eyes met and we exchanged subtle head nods. Everyone's facial expressions were earnest to the extreme.

After breakfast, I put on my kit. I made sure my vest was tight, grenades were secure, pistol was holstered with a round chambered, medical kit was in place, camelback was full, and I double checked that my radio was charged. I picked up my M21 rifle, which my team referred to as "Old Sarge." I gripped it with confidence and familiarity, made sure the scope was set to 500 meters, and that the scope caps were tight. I pulled the bolt back just enough to see a glimmer of shiny brass to ensure a round was chambered, and I made sure Old Sarge was on safe. My "kit" and weapon were a physical extension of my body and mind; I was a machine in this regard.

In accordance with the battle plan, my team had organized into four separate elements. Three of my teammates, one carrying a Barrett .50 caliber sniper rifle, were part of the Green Prong. The other part of my team organized into another three smaller groups and we constituted the Yellow Prong. I was the leader of one group of the three yellow prong elements, and my objective was to stay on the front line of the attack into Sargat. My Team Sergeant and one of my other teammates formed another Yellow Prong element, and their mission was also to push the front line with a different group of Kurds. My Captain, Uncle Andy, and some other CIA personnel constituted the command and control element. Each of our teams was going to integrate into a 500 to a 1000 strong Peshmerga force.

The mission of the yellow prong, and the purpose of Operation Viking Hammer, was to secure the Sargat Chemical Facility: a place that had gained national level interest because of its potential to tie Sadaam to Al Qaida, and because it was suspected to contain evidence of chemical weapons or poisons production. I couldn't believe I was finally part of something this big.[9]

I walked outside and glanced into the dark sky, then walked to the trucks through a crowd of hundreds of Kurds that were shining flashlights onto the tan colored dirt and concrete buildings inside the compound, chattering with one another in Kurdish as they prepared weapons and ammunition. We loaded our .50 caliber and MK19 along with tripods and ammo cans into the back of a small white pickup truck.[10] I boarded the back of another similar pickup truck that had small benches in the bed. I sat down, and placed Old Sarge's buttstock on the floor, barrel up, and squeezed it tightly with my famous black leather fingerless gloves that now had duct tape keeping the cutoff fingers from falling apart; the same gloves I was wearing that memorable day in Kosovo. I reflected on that experience for a second until the Kurdish driver started the truck and took off in the general direction of AAI's lair in the massive mountains that loomed in the distance. Along the bumpy road, I watched the outline of the dark, jagged mountains grow crisper against the sky as the sun rose behind them. My senses started to tingle as my nervousness increased.

As the truck grew closer to the small village of Dekon, and the sun had risen a bit more, a bewildering scene materialized before me as I squinted and peered into the distance through the dust from over the roof of the moving truck. I saw thousands of Peshmerga everywhere. A giant dark and tan blob of them sprawled for a mile wide across the sparsely grassed flatlands on the foothills of the snowcapped mountains that marked the Iranian border. The massive expanse of the Peshmerga horde was interspersed with hundreds of cars and trucks and other vehicles of all types, coming and going from as far as I could see in every direction. The cool breeze blew the rising dust, up and away, thousands of feet into the huge, orange, dawn sky above the sprawl of warriors. Belts of machine gun bullets and worn weapon's barrels reflected in the burgeoning sun and twinkled like space matter from within the giant cluster of Kurdish warriors.

As the truck grew closer, I was able to distinguish Peshmerga fighters of all ages pouring out of taxi cabs, overloaded small cars, pickup trucks, farming tractors, motorcycles, and all of them were wearing their best PUK Peshmerga attire. Some had pistols with fancy handles stuffed into their waistbands, most had AKs, but some had belt-fed machine guns, shotguns, or hunting rifles. Some had colorful bags or backpacks with embroidered flowers and other designs on them, and still others had brought the whole family along.

As I scanned the crowd of black and white checkered head wraps, baggy brown pants, and moustaches, I was confused by the presence of a few extra-large heavy construction style dump trucks. After I watched Peshmerga cram into the back of them, I realized that these dump trucks were actually Peshmerga *armored personnel carriers*. I also took special notice of a fascinating green flatbed truck, very large, about the size of a 2.5-ton Army truck. This truck had a giant two barreled anti-aircraft machine gun bolted to its bed, and it reminded me of a battleship. I also spotted many land rovers that had 106 MM recoilless rifles or Katoosha rocket pods mounted to them.

As we approached and then penetrated the edge of the Kurdish mass, the collective murmur of thousands of Peshmerga became audible, grew louder and louder, and then the smell of human feces mixed with dust and body odor became overwhelming. The Kurds cheered vigorously for us alongside the truck as we parted the sea of them, with their weapons raised into the air above intense dark eyes. I waved and smiled to them as the truck became surrounded and slowly crept towards the center of the sprawling Peshmerga horde.

The Kurdish leadership expected between eight and ten thousand Kurds to show up. I estimated that the crowd of Peshmerga covered at least one entire square mile, not counting the vehicles everywhere on the fringes. This War against AAI was like a community event to the PUK, and Kurds from all over Northeastern Iraq had hitched a ride any way they could to get there.

We got off the truck and found the Kurdish leaders that we would fight alongside. We also conversed randomly amongst ourselves to help cope with our nervousness. It wasn't long before the nervousness got the best of me, and I really needed to use a bathroom. Someone told me there was a small shed about 250 meters away through the crowd that was "the bathroom." I navigated through the crowd for a few minutes, and hundreds of smiling Kurds patted my back and admired the scope on my weapon. One Kurd said "I love your George Bush!" emphatically only inches from my face. Finally, I cut through the gracious and smelly crowd and made it to the shed.

When I opened the clumsy wooden door, I instantly knew the shed was the source of the intense fecal smell. There were two small mountains of human feces in the two back corners of the shed, and the holes in the floor were not even visible anymore. There was a metal rake leaned against the wall so people could make space to defecate by raking other people's feces to the corners. There were smear marks on the walls where the Kurds had wiped off their left hands. I used the rake to clear a spot and there was fecal matter on the handle, and I got some on my black leather gloves. I did my business and left as fast as I could; it was unbelievable, but I had bigger things to worry about.

It was full daylight when I walked out into the fresher air, and I reached down and grabbed some sand to clean my gloves. I instantly noticed that all the Kurds in my immediate vicinity were very intensely facing the mountains, and some murmured to each other in low serious voices without looking at each other. I curiously faced the mountains as well, to see what they were all looking at. I saw the dark silhouettes of AAI fighters along the first ridgeline watching us with defiance, and I instantly knew why everyone looked so solemn. The scene reminded me of the movie Braveheart, where the two enemies faced off before battle, and like the movie, we were just waiting for a signal to begin the charge.

I made my way back through the crowd to where my team was, and my Captain told me there were aircraft inbound to "prep" the front ridgeline ("prep" is a fancy military term for bombing the hell out of somewhere before you go in). As the sound of the approaching aircraft became audible in the distance, I watched the AAI fighters run back off the ridge out of my view, just before the ridgeline burst into violent explosions as three or four large bombs dropped in succession along the crest. The ethereal boom of the thunderous explosions shook the earth and sent a tingling shock through my body, and the crowd of Peshmerga cheered vigorously, at least until the AAI fighters reappeared on the ridge not more than a minute later. The AAI were not distinguishable as anything more than dark abstract anthropomorphic shapes due to the distance, but I could feel that they had no fear.

At that moment, a fear arose that I had never felt before. The feeling was the uniquely primitive brand of fear that settles in when a person realizes that another group of human beings wants to kill them.[11]

A Peshmerga man in his 40s, who had his weapon slung and wore a typical pair of tan baggy Peshmerga pants climbed up the side of the battleship truck, which was now completely encircled by hundreds of restless Peshmerga. He expertly manipulated the creaky cranks and wheels until the massive cannon pointed in the direction of the AAI figures on the ridge. The barrels of the weapon were probably ten feet long, and they both had large cylinders on the ends that looked like giant silencers.

The Kurd fired the weapon, and my ears instantly rang from the noise. The cannon made an exceptionally loud disturbing metal-on-metal grating sound when it fired. The sharp repetitive bark of the weapon rolled like thunder towards the mountains, and then echoed back as a wispier tone. The unnatural smell of gunpowder from the cannon mingled with the smell of human feces and body odor, and then drifted over the murmuring horde in the cool breeze. The battleship's tracers looked like glowing weightless softballs as they flew towards the ridge. I assumed the battleship was firing flak rounds because the rounds exploded in the air above the ridge. The cannon fired so fast and powerfully, and it rocked the truck back and forth so violently, that the surrounding Peshmerga horde rippled as hundreds of men recoiled from around it. The battleship made the AAI Fighters scramble, and again dozens of their dark forms disappeared over the ridge.

The firing of the battleship was the signal to charge. The Peshmerga mob stirred, and their chatter grew louder as my heartrate surged in anticipation. The handful of Green Berets, CIA, and Air Force Operators, dispersed among the unorganized line of trucks and the crowd of rag-bag Kurdish warriors, began to ooze towards the mountains, compelled by an unspoken force of energy and unity. As I advanced among a sea of fighters, a low and gruff war cry began to emulate from the masses. It was like how the men in Braveheart yelled as they began to charge the enemy, except we were all carrying rifles and machine guns instead of broad swords and battle axes.

I jumped into the back of a light pickup truck as it crept towards the enemy. From my elevated position in the back of the pickup, I was floating on top of an impetuous tan colored sea of weapon clad Peshmerga wearing black and white head wraps, all of whom were trotting, elbow to elbow, eyes trained on AAI's mountain stronghold. Some AAI fighters were running along the ridge. Soon there were more Kurds firing the 106s, and the battleship continued to fire over our heads onto the ridge to help secure our approach to the valley entrance.

We reached a destroyed AAI checkpoint and the Green Prong branched off, as planned, and they hustled towards the ridgeline to my left. I wished them well, and I watched my teammates walk straight up the enormous ridge distributed among their Peshmerga until they became indistinguishable shapes among their horde. I continued forward towards the opening of the valley, and then I heard the Green Prong come under fire, which made the hair stand up on the back of my neck because I knew it wouldn't be long until we made contact as well.

We continued towards the mouth of the Sargat valley, and drove by one of the checkpoints that we had observed so many times during Advanced Force Operations. There was a burnt and now rotting lower leg laying on the ground with the jagged tibia completely exposed. The foot was still wearing a boot, and there was shredded skin, meat, and shards of clothing attached. The Kurds kicked the rotting human leg out of the way emotionlessly as we all continued to move forward another couple hundred meters. There were around 1500 Kurds spread out behind and in front of me when we finally stopped. I dismounted and glanced in the direction of the sound of the Green Prong's sporadic firing.

I moved rapidly on foot along the windy dirt road, a mere speck within the enormity of the Peshmerga crowd, careful not to venture into the long grass because the Kurds had told us prior that there were landmines, which made me perceive the grass as frightening and unnatural. As I walked up the valley among the mass of Peshmerga towards the enemy my sense of imminent danger increased with each step.

I continued around the bend and finally the great expanse of the Sargat valley extended before me. To my left I saw a blur of rough green and brown grass extending for thousands of yards along a massive bald ridge with jagged rocks strewn all over the place. The bombs that were dropped a few minutes prior had perverted the landscape, thrown blackened rocks everywhere, and sent a burnt ozone smell into the air. To my front, the narrow, light-brown, dirt road slithered up the sparsely grassy and rocky valley floor up and through a small village called Gulp, which was about one kilometer away. The village had jagged but beautiful layers of snowcapped mountains far behind its primitive outline. These mountains marked the Iranian border, and essentially comprised the finish line for this attack; which looked like a hundred miles away. To my right I observed a small knoll with a few small shrub-like trees on top and some piles of rocks. I was glad that I brought Old Sarge and not my M4 carbine as I gazed across the expansive terrain.

I made radio contact with my company mortar team as I continuously scanned the hills to my front along with the horde that surrounded me. I was encircled by a whirling blur of tan MC Hammer pants, thick black moustaches, white and black head wraps, the yellow glistening of belts of machine gun bullets, the rattle of weapons, the smell of body odor, and incessant nervous chatter in Kurdish. My senses were overloaded by the size of the terrain, the crowd of smelly warriors chattering and clattering around me, and the sound of pitched shouting and machine gun fire from the Green prong to my left. So far, this attack was everything I had dreamed it would be.

Suddenly, AAI machine gun fire erupted from my right and front simultaneously. It was like the world around me instantly froze, and then became a mirror that shattered into fractals of confusion and sunlight and sky and blue and green as I searched for cover. The Peshmerga began sprinting toward the sound of machine gun fire, and their murmuring turned into frantic shouting as bullets snapped overhead and weapons fire echoed around me. My heart rate and nerves surged. There was nowhere to take cover. I was on an open road in an open valley, with possible landmines off the road. That feeling of nakedness and doom that I had felt a few days prior when that mortar almost hit me swept over me again.

I jumped down into the prone position in a small rut on the side of the road, a pathetic attempt at cover, relieved that I hadn't exploded due to a landmine, and began to scan the knoll to the right through my rifle's scope to try and identify where the fire was coming from. I could see the Peshmerga on the offensive, already at the bottom of the knoll, running in a swarm towards the firing. I spotted what looked like an AAI Fighter near a pile of rocks, but I could not confirm well enough that it was not a Kurd. The Peshmerga were moving so fast that they could have made it there by then, so I didn't take the shot.

Bullets were flying everywhere. Tracers bounced off the hillsides and dirt around me. The Kurds continued to spread out in flanking operations, having no choice but to accept the risk of landmines and venture off the road.

I began to run towards Gulp with my three-man team to the front line of our Kurds, but slowed down, looked up, and scanned the sky when I heard the rapidly growing sound of a Jet flying at low altitude, approaching from behind us. All the Peshmerga around me intensely scanned the sky with both fear and awe in their concentrated eyes, mouths agape under dark moustaches. As the aircraft grew rapidly closer, it sounded like a knife was ripping through the atmosphere like it was a giant piece of heavy blue canvas. The ear-piercing sound of the jet grew even more colossal and unnatural when the pilot fired a massive burst from the aircraft's main machine gun at the hillside just beyond Gulp. The hillside burst into dust as if it had erupted instantly, and I felt each of the hundreds of small explosions in my gut. I instinctually crouched in response to the devastation I had just witnessed as I ran towards Gulp. The AAI fire stopped, and the Kurds and I cheered triumphantly; The motivational effect of the airstrike was instantly realized. The Peshmerga horde, and I among them, sprinted and screamed towards Gulp as the noise of the aircraft faded and became a background tone for the Kurdish chatter and battle rattle that surrounded me.

The magnitude of the scene was almost imperceptible as I ran along the road. Thousands of Kurdish fighters ran and yelled towards the hills, the sound of machine gun fire was omnipresent, aircraft streaked overhead, the smell of burnt ground and body odor mixed with machine gun grease flooded my flared nostrils, wounded Peshmerga limped past me, and the Kurds were thoroughly distributed across the vast terrain like locusts.[12],[13]

We made it to Gulp, and I stopped and stood next to a very old stone Mosque; the one I had seen from a distance. The Mosque had two holes in its roof, and I caught a glimpse of dead bodies on the inside through some openings in the primitive outer walls. In close vicinity to the Mosque, there were several dead AAI bodies on the ground. Blood trails from the bodies steamed in the cold morning air and ran like small rivers through the micro terrain near each corpse. I picked up one of the Radical Islamic teaching books that were scattered around the outside of the mosque. The cover had Arabic writing on it, and pictures of British and American flags burning with the Twin Towers smoking in the background.

The vehicles caught up with us, and we miraculously united with our truck that had our heavy weapons in the back, so I jumped into the back and we continued to advance towards Sargat. At Gulp, one large group of Peshmerga broke off and followed another Green Beret team (the Red prong) south, and another large horde continued with us. As we drove out of Gulp, I swallowed dust, inhaled the burnt air, and continued to look at the motionless dead bodies until they were out of site, masked by terrain.

We started receiving fire from a valley to our south and rounds pinged off the earth and stones around our truck. We all jumped out and I tried to locate the source of the fire, which I failed to do. I got frustrated because this was the second time we'd taken fire, and the second time I had been unsuccessful at identifying exactly where it was coming from. The terrain was incredibly huge and mostly light brown, with small tads of green, so the tan uniforms of the AAI fighters blended in well.[14]

My Team Sergeant spotted them, and he told us to pull the MK19 off the truck and set it up. I faced up the hill to our east in case we were attacked from over the hill. He fired the MK19 for about 50 or so rounds and the AAI fire stopped. Either the AAI who were shooting at us died, or they ran away, or the advancing Kurds to our south took them out.

None of us knew that the Green and Red prongs were flushing the bulk of the AAI fighters into Sargat. We were about to hit hundreds of them head on.

We quickly threw the MK19 in the truck, I jumped in the back again, and we kept moving forward. I could not see Sargat yet, but I knew it was right around the corner. Prior to the Attack during all the preparations, and because of all the intelligence we had collected on the AFO mission, my mind had constructed a vision of Sargat as some kind of evil medieval fortress or demonic monster, so my anxiety surged as I got closer. My small team and I dismounted and continued on foot among the Kurds.

In the distance across the valley, along the ridge, I saw the Green Prong's horde fighting their way forward along the high ground. I knew my teammates were amongst the mass of advancing human forms, and to myself I wished them luck. The gunfire, explosions, smoke, and Kurdish yelling increased in volume continuously as we progressed further east.

I rounded a corner caused by a spur in the terrain, and there were tracers flying and ricocheting everywhere. Dozens of Kurds screamed at us to get down with crazed intensity in their eyes and we ran for cover. One of my teammates had the M240 machine gun and a few Kurds helped us with ammo. We ran forward to where a cluster of Peshmerga was pinned down along the road, and I focused my vision intensely on the foot of the ridge on the other side of the valley where the majority of fire seemed to be coming from. I could have run one hundred miles because of the adrenaline.

We ran through a light sprinkling of snapping tracers until we found cover behind a very small finger that extended into the valley. The streaming tracer bullets that were accompanied by snapping sounds kept me low as we set up the M240 and I started spotting for AAI. There were a few AAI below a rocky part of the Green Prong's ridge about 300 meters away, firing up at the Green Prong as they advanced. All the Kurds around me fired into the same area, but their fire was not very effective. My teammate unleashed a hail of fire with the M240, and the AAI dispersed a bit while I scanned with Old Sarge.

Through my scope, I saw a bearded AAI fighter moving backwards, and firing upwards at members of the Green prong. I placed my mil dot crosshairs on his tan waist. At this range, since my sight was set to 500 I knew that aiming at his waist would put the round in the chest area. My training took over and I became super calm for a second, I completely ignored the chaos of war around me, and became hyper-aware of my own breathing.

I inhaled then slowly exhaled, and when my breath was almost all the way out, I carefully and smoothly squeezed the trigger. The rifle fired, and the round was on its way. Since I was in a steady position, my rifle's recoil did not kick enough to take my aim off the AAI fighter, and I watched him falter and fall to the ground, then crawl down the hill into some light trees or shrubbery. I fired a few more rounds in succession and he stopped moving.[15]

The noise of war flooded back into my ringing ears and I realized that I lost sight of my Team Sergeant, as well as my Captain. I quickly assumed they were engaged somewhere else, so it was just my three-man team amongst a several hundred strong Peshmerga group. Our Kurds received a signal to move, likely by cell phone, or maybe pure instinct, so we started moving rapidly forward on the front line of the attack into Sargat.

My team and I jogged down the sparely grassed hill, off the road and onto the rocky and grassy valley floor along with our group of several hundred Kurds. Fifty or so Peshmerga were in my immediate vicinity, along with hundreds more slightly ahead and behind me in clear view. An old man of about 70 years old gave me a giant toothless grin and a big thumbs-up as he walked along with an AK in one hand and a cane in another.

As we continued incessantly forward, the tracer fire increased, and the mind shattering sound of combat became ubiquitous and grew towards a crescendo. The Green Prong was heavily engaged, and I actually heard the distinct bark of that Barrett .50 cal reverberate periodically. Mortars exploded, RPGs sizzled through the air, and tracers flew everywhere once I rounded the huge corner of the valley and cast my eyes upon the objective.

Sargat was a primitive, shamble of concrete dwellings sparsely interspersed with skinny wilted trees; eerily dark even under the clear midday sky. It looked like a giant bowl had been tilted towards me, with a rim made of massive olive and brown ridgelines. The back side of the bowl, which extended from beyond the main cluster of disorganized structures, was horizontally striped with enormous and twisted tendril-like lines of ledge. Nestled into the shadows of the tentacles were dozens of crooked grey concrete building structures, semi-organic to the ledges they were under, each with their own form, with black windowless openings that looked like empty black eyes. The tendrils looked like they were bleeding due to the erosion of reddish soil that was layered into the ledge outcroppings. The angle of the sun on the jagged ledges casted long lines of gloomy shadows down the steep hillsides. The occasional flashes of AAI weapon's fire from within the black eyes made them seem alive and mystical.

In the distance, birds flew fitfully from some of the sickly trees as explosions startled them, and they looked like mere specs in contrast to the unimaginable scale of the terrain and geography around them. The rows of menacing white mountain peaks along the Iranian border loomed behind Sargat and projected a sense of governance over everything in the expanse below them. I felt impossibly small and insignificant as I jogged up the valley floor towards the sound of machine gun fire in a semi crouch as bullets snapped and whizzed by me.

The span of green valley that led into Sargat had staggered layers of stone walls running across it at random intervals. These stone walls were the only cover or concealment available except for a small ravine that was a thousand meters ahead of us. I didn't have time to perceive any more of the scene to fully orient myself, because I immediately began receiving an unimaginable volume of gun fire from our 10 and 12 o'clock. I sprinted through snapping tracers towards the protection of the nearest row of stone walls and dove down behind one. I still had no idea where my Team Sergeant and Captain were, which had me concerned, but I knew where my team was, and that we had a job to do: keep bounding forward with the front line and take the village.

As we fired and maneuvered from one stone wall to the next, one of the guys on my team fell and badly smashed his knee but kept going forward. With the amount of tracer fire, and other munitions exploding everywhere, it was nearly impossible to locate any AAI fighters to fire at. There were Kurds everywhere firing alongside us, and I was almost killed by a Kurdish machine gunner when I moved laterally to get to another stone wall; he smiled and nodded to me apologetically even though we both knew it was my fault. Mortars landed violently with intense concussion, earth upheaved, RPGs streamed through the air, and the three of us finished another sprint and made it to another wall. We smiled at each other and exchanged some comedic comments about what a nice day it was.

I attempted continuously to spot targets and fire at AAI from behind the wall. In one case, like a fool, I did not have my barrel above the stone wall, only my scope, and my round hit the wall right in front of my barrel when I fired. One of the guys on my team yelled "I saw that!" It was embarrassing, but I was too scared to care. The Kurds had staged the trucks along the road to our 4 o'clock, and one of the trucks had a 106MM recoilless rifle mounted on it.

The 106 had no sights on it, so to aim it, I watched the Peshmerga gunner open the breach, look through the barrel from back to front, and then move the gun until his target was in the center of the tube. He had so much experience with firing the weapon without real sights that he knew how to adjust for elevation based on his estimation of the distance. I heard him firing the cannon repeatedly over the other noise as we fought our way deeper into the valley toward Sargat, bounding from one row of stone walls to another under intense fire. My eyes darted from point to point with such rapidity that my senses couldn't process the changing images fast enough, and for a while it was as if I couldn't see anything at all.

My senses and fear were so inflated from the perpetual uncertainty of death, and primitive state of survival that swept over me, that my ability to smell became animalistic. There was a heavy earthy and grassy smell in the air because of the dirt the mortar rounds were upheaving. The smell of the oil and carbon from my rifle, my black leather gloves, my breath, the smoke of munitions in the air, my sweat, and the crispness of the cool morning air were so strong I could taste them. The sounds were even more exaggerated than the smells. The rockets streaking, mortars tearing through the sky, the snap of bullets over my head, the bark of my own rifle, the deafening sound of the 106s, Kurdish machine gun fire, distressed Kurdish chatter, distant and near enemy machine gun fire which was correlated to the snapping sound over my head like the two were in harmony, and the ringing in my ears were all echoing back and forth in the valley and in my head, growing and growing with such intensity I thought the entire valley would detonate into oblivion.[16]

I popped my head up to scan for AAI, and in slow motion, a tracer left the edge of one of the buildings on the outskirts of Sargat and whizzed just past the right side of my head with a snap. Every time I tried to locate any AAI from behind the wall in order to engage with my rifle, bullets streaked by my head and slammed into the wall in front of me with inconceivable force.

An unbounded and increasing stream of tracers poured over the stone wall, and bullets continued to slap into it. I looked down along the stone wall that extended to my left where my other two teammates were in the prone along with dozens of Peshmerga that had spread out between and beyond them. They popped up and down as they struggled to engage AAI, and tracers streamed past them all in depth.

We struggled like this for several hours; an eternity, trying with futility to locate and accurately fire back at AAI while taking heavy fire, until finally, as I scrambled around behind the walls, one of my teammates shouted to me, eyes full of bewilderment *"what the fuck are we going to do!?"* I tried to get a hold of the mortar team, but I could not reach them anymore. I tried to call my Captain, but I couldn't reach him either.

I had no idea what to do and I felt completely isolated; miniscule and helpless in the face of our situation, massively disappointed in myself. I thought to myself over and over.

I am a Green Beret. I am supposed to know what to do.

Within 30 seconds of primitive mental churn, options started to materialize in my sub-conscience while I tried to ignore the ambient sounds of war and the constant interruption of bullets ricocheting off the wall in front of me.

We could not move forward, because I didn't know where any of the AAI fighters really were. We'd have been shot instantly because of the sheer volume of fire and because there wasn't any more cover until we made it inside Sargat. Moving to the left made no sense, because there were no stonewalls there, and that meant no cover. There was no doubt that we had to move, and it appeared that to the right presented the highest probability of survival.

As my mind churned and I prepared myself to move, a new, very low, ominous sound joined the valley's war symphony. This sound was so deep and profound, it was like belt-fed thunder, it seemed to command the lesser sounds of war in the valley. This new sound originated from a very large heavy machine gun on the huge ridge to the east above Sargat, and it was mowing down the valley floor from an unknown AAI position.

The reality that the instrument which produced this new sound could at any nanosecond render me shredded to pieces on that valley floor, elicited an epic feeling of absolute and pervasive doom from within an unfamiliar and primitive place within my soul. A heavy feeling swept over me like a black tidal wave, and joined with the feeling of disappointment in myself; I had never imagined such a feeling of oppression and imminent doom was possible. I was convinced that I was going to die, and I froze; I had no idea what to do.

Out of nowhere, through a horizontal rain of tracers, my Captain sprinted over to me from somewhere to my right and dove down beside me; his sudden presence confirmed my suspicion that we were in deep trouble. He asked me, yelling over the noise, if we were doing ok, and he told me there was cover to our right. As he sprinted away, half crouched, through a hail of bullets, I suddenly felt a rush of motivation; he inspired me. He had left his laminated and folded map on the ground next to me, and just as I picked it up, he came bouncing back over to get it. I said "hey sir, I would have brought you your map, don't get yourself killed!"

My small team and I conversed briefly by shouting to each other over the incessant sounds of war, and decided to move to the right or we were doomed. I also very suddenly decided that these extremists were not going to deprive me of seeing my newborn baby daughter and my wife again, and that was when the fear in my mind transformed to fury and hate, perhaps evil, like water suddenly reaching a rolling boil. I felt like a swarm of emboldened atoms rather than a man, superhuman, with no emotion or sympathy for any life on earth other than my own or my team's. This rage was what I needed. So, with a newfound level of primal aggression, I told my team to start bounding to the right, and I prepared to move.

I got up and started running. I perceived an increase in the snapping sound of the bullets flying by me, the volume of my own heartbeat increased, and my own pulse rushed through my ears as I saw muzzle flashes out of the corners of both eyes. Everything was a blur, but within a few seconds, through the mist of my own kaleidoscopic perception, a small tunnel of clarity appeared ahead, and through this tunnel I saw a small gathering of people huddled behind a slightly higher portion of stone wall approximately 100 meters away. When I initially jumped up and ran, I had no idea where I was going, but now I had a specific destination.

After almost getting shot again by another Kurd who was behind a wall that I ran in front of, I dropped down behind another wall. When I got down AAI concentrated fire at the wall where they had seen me disappear, and I cursed out loud in response. I crawled about 20 feet, then popped up and made another final dash through the tracers until I reached the cluster of people behind the cover of the larger chunk of stone wall. I was relieved that I made it, and soon my other two teammates joined us.

My Captain, Uncle Andy, Bafel Talibani, and one of our interpreters were all there behind the wall. Bafel was talking to his father, Jalal Talibani (the future president of Iraq) on a satellite phone. His dad was mad at him for participating in the battle and putting himself in such danger. Uncle Andy, who probably read the shell shocked look of fury on my face, told me this was the last time he would ever go on an operation with a bunch of crazy Green Berets; he was joking.

I spotted a few fleeting AAI Fighters about 250 meters away on the other side of a few buildings, and I shot at them, but I couldn't confirm whether it was my bullets that wounded them or someone else's.[17] The ominous sound of the Heavy AAI machine gun continued as my Captain and Uncle Andy conversed by shouting in each other's ears over the noise.

They said we needed to get the .50 cal on to the high ground, to take out AAI's heavy machine gun.

My Captain told my team to make it happen.

The .50 cal was in the back of a pickup, and all the pickups were lined up 400 meters away to our 3 o'clock. I took a nervous deep breath, looked across the expanse of terrain and the density of tracers flying across it, then exhaled shakily. My whole body tightened as I peered across four football fields of streaming tracers that I was about to run through to get to those trucks.

All three of us simultaneously ran out into the pouring tracers; I felt like I broke the barrier to another dimension when I left the protection of the stone wall. As I ran, there were hundreds of Kurds firing past us and we continuously yelled to make sure they saw us coming so we didn't get shot by friendly fire. Heavy lines of tracers flew past me in both directions, like a laser light show, and bullets struck the ground and hills everywhere. I was so tense, braced in anticipation for the impact of a bullet, I felt as if my muscles might rip out of my skin. A large caliber tracer struck a washed-out embankment and ricocheted upwards, spinning very fast like some kind of firework. It arced over our heads and we ran under it like a ring of fire. We were in awesome physical condition, so the sprint didn't bother us, even though we were each carrying about 50 pounds of kit.

Finally, huffing and puffing, but extremely focused and unimaginably furious, I reached a white Nissan truck. One of my teammates jumped in the driver's seat, I got into the passenger seat, and another jumped in the back. Just as I sat down and the vehicle lurched forward into the flurry of bullets, a bullet penetrated the front windshield with a pop and a zing and went out the open door next to me; it passed right in front of my face. My teammate floored it and we drove for about 300 meters until we turned up a very small trail and stopped. I dismounted.

There was a huge green hill to my front, which completely blocked my view of Sargat. On my left, I could still see the valley of Kurds being oppressed by a relentless volley of tracers. We needed to bring the .50 cal machine gun, and a sufficient amount of ammo, to the top of this hill. I smelled the earth and grass, and then the terrifying sound of AAI's heavy machine gun spoke again as I reached the bed of the truck to get the .50 cal. My teammate, our communications sergeant, a beast of a man, grabbed the 80 plus pound machine gun and easily hoisted it onto his shoulder, prepared to run up the hill with it. My other teammate grabbed the tripod for it, which was also at least 20 pounds. I slung Old Sarge and grabbed 2 ammo cans, and so did a half a dozen Peshmerga who showed up to help.

We sprinted up the massive ridge, 300 meters to get to the top along a 45 degree or steeper angle. We charged upwards like machines, like Olympians with guns, on a mission to dominate the valley and get out alive. I dug the toes of my boots so furiously into the grass and dirt as I powered up the hill that I could feel individual small pebbles through the soles, and I breathed mechanically with each stride.[18]

I reached the crest of the hill and my thighs were pumped and my heart was almost exploding in my chest. Miraculously, I spotted a divot in the ground on the top of the ridge. The ridge was completely bald, green, and rounded on the top, and this divot enabled us to set up the .50 cal and have a small amount of protection. I was able to see the entire expanse of Sargat. From on top of the ridge, my eyes rendered the dark scene below me like an abstract painting that was alive with violence.

We crawled up and got into the divot, which was only about a foot deep. I saw a Kurd get shredded by machine gun fire on the front side of the hill as his group tried to advance from the south; he was sickeningly dismantled as tracers passed through his body. I also identified the Sargat Chemical Facility compound for the first time; our objective. It was right below our position on the ridge. I recognized it because I had memorized the overhead imagery prior.

From up there on that ridge, the sound of war in the valley had a different feel to it, more ambient with more reverb, but louder, as if the valley was boiling over with noise, a cacophony of death. The sounds of war are unforgettable, especially the coalesced sound of screaming human voices, loaded with such an abnormally high amount of agony, fear, stress, and urgency. From the divot, I scanned the bowl and searched for the location of AAI's machine gun.

I quickly identified a dark grey concrete structure with a single black opening that lit up as large tracers flew from it. I knew It was where the heavy machine gun was. My teammates had already set up the .50 cal on its tripod, and it was ready for action. I pointed out the building to my team, which was probably 600 meters away. My communications guy didn't hesitate and began firing the .50, which increased the noise in the valley tenfold. We immediately came under fire in response, and I slid down as low as I could into the divot. I laid my weapon on its side so I could stay low and still look through the scope sideways. My teammate walked his .50 cal tracers onto the flashing building, and I helped feed ammo from the different ammo cans. My fear was that we would not destroy their gun before AAI got on target with us; it was like a duel, so we had to be quick. Soon we were absolutely shredding the structure, and we just kept hammering it until we had fired about 600 rounds into it. As my teammate fired, I looked through my scope and saw our bullets actually passing *through* the structure. The AAI tracers stopped emitting, and the building stopped flashing.

They Kurds below us began to advance when we started firing. The Peshmerga stampede flooded the perimeter of the evil fortress of Sargat and swept through it like ants suddenly rushing through the paths of a large and complex ant farm. I glanced at the now dark and empty AAI machine gun structure one last time before we packed up the .50 cal and ran down off the hill rapidly. We went through the ruins of the chemical facility, careful not to touch the extremely hot barrel of the .50 cal. When we got to the bottom, and linked up with my Captain, the strangest thing happened.[19]

The Kurds brought us assorted meats on what looked like a silver platter. It was lunch time.

We ate our lunch quickly from behind a berm on the side of a road that had been carved out of the ridge, within a few feet from the poison and chemical facility, which looked like a pile of rubble with some remaining structure and a fence around it. A fairly consistent trickle of tracers still flew and snapped overhead. There was still fighting going on, but it appeared that the bulk of the work to take Sargat was over and the Kurds had it covered. While we ate, several truckloads of wounded and dead Kurds that were being moved back to Halabja drove by. One such truck, which in its bed carried a pile of about 10 Kurd's bodies, stopped next to us and our medic examined a disfigured man who had been shot in the leg, face, and shoulder. As they drove away, human blood ran from the bed of the truck like a thick crimson waterfall, and my stomach knotted at the sight of so much human blood.

We finished eating quickly, thanked the Kurds, and began to drive around the south side of Sargat, past and away from the mystical chemical factory. We drove around the southern perimeter of Sargat to a very rough road that climbed the steep terrain along switchbacks very near to where that heavy machine gun was. As I looked down the hill across the expanse of Sargat, I was stunned by the sheer volume of dead bodies everywhere. There was a body every 10 or 15 feet, motionless in unnatural positions for almost as far as I could see. The sound of war echoed from a riverbed to my left as we climbed the rough mountain switchbacks.

We finally reached a plateau, and I saw a few buildings in the distance from the back of the truck. We had two or three land rovers and trucks, one of them had a 106MM recoilless rifle mounted on it. As we got closer, we stopped the vehicles on the outer edge of a cluster of dilapidated concrete buildings, dismounted, and continued on foot to clear this relatively small area.

As we approached the shoddy buildings, I realized how high we had climbed into the mountains, and how massive the white snowcapped peaks were along the Iranian border. There were no AAI fighters in the buildings, so we moved some of the vehicles closer. We had 15 or so people with us; Uncle Andy, Bafel Talibani, my team, an interpreter, and a group of Peshmerga surrounded me.

As we reached the easternmost building, just as we thought everything was clear, we started receiving withering machine gun fire from a ridge directly in front of us. We all jumped down behind a building, which the AAI machine guns incessantly chipped away at, and I was again astonished and terrified by the sheer force of the bullets' impact.

That same black wave of doom and helplessness swept over me again when I realized that this battle wasn't over, and we were in big trouble again.

Bullets slapped and ricocheted off the building at an alarming rate. Rounds struck the ground and streamed by each side of the building. I was concerned that there might be another group of AAI advancing on us under the cover of the machine gun fire. We couldn't just sit there and allow ourselves to get surprised, and the Kurds knew this. They started running over to the 106 truck to return fire. I moved to the left side of the building, laid as flat as I could to minimize exposure, and looked through my scope to see if I could identify the source of the fire. Nothing but rocks became apparent to me, and again I was brutally irritated that the firing was too intense for me to get a decent look at anything. It was like fighting against ghosts.

Grit and my medic crawled up next to me, and they put the .50 cal into operation. The machine gun fire came from a ridge that ran perpendicular to the way we were facing, and I saw a few AAI fighters dashing around the rocks on the ridge to our front. I fired at them, and I startled and agitated Grit as he tried to get the .50 set up. I could not tell if I hit anything, but I just continued to lay down fire because I thought it might cause some of them to move, and then we'd at least be able to locate them.

Grit fired the .50, and as soon as he did, the AAI machine gun fire increased. I ran backwards to a position behind the 106 truck, where I huddled tightly next to Bafel against the tailgate, where we both crouched helplessly as bullets pinged off the truck almost musically and kicked up dirt all around us. I looked down and to my right as I crouched, and saw bullets hitting the soft dirt just a few inches away from my foot; I was terrified as I imagined those bullets tearing through my soft flesh and bone if they shifted over just a few inches. A Kurd ran over and loaded the 106 and prepared to fire. Based on the way he was talking and pointing I assumed he had identified a target. The 106's breach was right above my head; I was crouched under it. The concussion alone from a 106 can be dangerous, and I braced myself as the Kurd slammed a shell into the breach, closed it, and prepared to fire; he was fearless.[20], [21]

The Kurd fired the 106 and the blast wave rippled through my entire body and my brain jiggled in my skull. I had fired a 106 before many times so at least I wasn't surprised by the force of the blast. We were in this situation for several minutes, the gunner continuously fired the 106 from over my head, and the ringing in my ears and pain in my body grew with each blast. Grit had abandoned the .50, and I was not sure where they were. After a few more 106 rounds, I was almost completely deafened, my whole body ached, and I ran back behind one of the buildings through a stream of tracers.

As we sprinted back to take cover, my Captain told us that an aircraft was inbound to provide air support. My medic, who we called "Hap," severely burned his hand on the .50 cal barrel as we dashed backwards. As I ran back to take new cover, rounds struck the ground just in front of me, and also splashed up dirt just behind Bafel's feet as we sprinted through tracer fire.

I very suddenly started to grow massively fatigued and downright ill; breathing was difficult, and I grew nauseous. My Captain yelled into the radio, and then I heard a Jet tearing through the sky again overhead, approaching rapidly from the south. Just as my Captain told the pilot to go ahead and drop the bombs, and the jet's noise grew to a shivering climax, a large group of Kurds from the Green Prong suddenly materialized from over the ridge from the north; the same ridge that he had just directed the pilot to drop bombs on. They were headed towards the kill zone!

We all winced as the pilot dropped bombs across the face of the ridge at "danger close" range to us; no more than 400 meters away. The Green Prong had made it even further across the target area of the ridge.

Boom, Boom, Boom, Boom!

The earth shook like a localized earthquake, I could feel the concussion cut through my bones and every organ in my body, and the ringing in my ears grew even louder due to the thunderous, earth shuddering crack of the explosions. I watched from the corner of the building as the mushroom-like explosions detonated near our Green Prong members; so close that the dust and black smoke from the blasts instantly covered them from view. They were *so* close I assumed many of them had to have been killed. I looked at my Captain and his face was made of stone. The wind blew the giant plumes of black smoke slowly to my left in front of the snowy peaks.

Suddenly there was an omnipresent sound of massive amounts of mortar rounds or artillery rounds, screaming and falling through the sky from what seemed like every direction. My blood ran cold as I thought either AAI still had copious mortar tubes somewhere, or that perhaps the Iranians decided to take sides against us (I could see one of their checkpoints from where we were).

One of the Kurds said something that I did not understand. Bafel translated for us and said "Rocks!" The sounds of mortars and artillery that I thought I heard were actually the sound of *rocks* that had been launched into the sky at high velocity by the explosive power of the four large bombs that were just dropped.

The AAI machine gun fire stopped. My Captain immediately called the Green Prong, and it turned out that miraculously no one was killed that they knew of. It was almost a major friendly fire incident.[22]

The Green Prong Kurds swept southeast along the freshly bombed ridge. They avoided the black scorched holes in the earth that the bombs had created. Their small forms moved so quickly across the rough terrain that from my vantage point they seemed like tiny figurines. There was a bit of sporadic firing, but since the bombs had taken care of most of the AAI there; the firing we heard was just the Kurds making sure the AAI bodies they encountered were dead.

I grew more and more ill by the minute; we'd been fighting since dawn. I had developed a splitting headache and incredible lethargy.[23] We packed everything up, and then began to discuss what we should do next. A small group of Kurds came down the hill behind us in a vehicle and told us they had found some kind of missiles in a position on a hill. Grit and another guy went to investigate with the Kurds, and quickly came back with information that they had found some very large French made missiles. The missiles were still in the cases.

We were almost completely out of .50 cal ammunition, we were all down to only a few magazines, and it was getting dark. The Kurds are not night fighters for the most part, at least not in rural areas, so we all decided to call it a night and head back down to Sargat to find a place to spend the night. The way I felt, I was glad to call it a day after more than 16 hours of fighting.

As we reentered Sargat, I was stunned to see that Kurds had already occupied most of the village. I saw a few women sweeping out houses and getting ready to move their families into them; they waved and smiled to us thankfully. Kids were already playing outside in some areas, ignoring the dead bodies everywhere. I realized we had just liberated a very large area of Kurdistan from these AAI Extremists. The Kurds were making piles of dead AAI bodies in various places, and their estimates were that we killed at least 300 of them. They wouldn't tell us how many Kurds were wounded or killed.

There were massive amounts of captured AAI information and equipment. The Kurds consolidated it all into the back of pickups and dump trucks. We found a house in the center of the village and hunkered down for the night. Everyone chatted a bit about each other's experiences before going to sleep. Grit's small team had been in serious trouble much like mine had. The medic with Grit had tried to patch up a Kurd whose intestines were hanging out, and there were many other details exchanged. Again, similar to how everyone felt after that battle in Kosovo, everyone felt like they had finally become a real warrior. I felt so bad I just tried to sleep.

The next morning, still feeling awful, I awoke to find our Battalion and Group commander had arrived at our house in Sargat. Colonel Cleveland and Ltc Tovo had come out to see how we were doing and congratulate us on a job well done. We shook hands and I gave Col Cleveland a man hug. I had known Col Cleveland for quite some time, he was my Battalion commander on my trip to Bihać Bosnia, and I'd always had a good rapport with him. We told them our stories, they patted our backs, and they told us what was going on in the big picture of the war. Soon they left, but their acknowledgment and opinion that we had done a good job made our spirits soar. Not for long in my case.[24]

After Tovo and Cleveland departed, a Sensitive Site Exploitation (SSE) team arrived to look for evidence of chemical weapons production in the Sargat chemical facility. Some of the members of this SSE team wore those silver shiny chemical protective suits. As we watched them, we half-jokingly asked ourselves why weren't *we* wearing these shiny space suits the day prior as we walked through and then ate lunch right next to the chemical facility? What kind of intelligence had these guys received that we didn't? Having no alternative, I brushed it off and escorted them to the facility, then poked around for a while with them in the cool early morning air. There were scattered stones, rubble, and equipment everywhere.

A representative from the SSE team said they needed hair samples from the dead AAI fighters, because hair sample analysis would be one of the ways to prove whether AAI had been performing chemical and poison engineering in the facility. This request trickled down to my medic and I, and we were told to go cut hair samples from the dead AAI bodies that were littered throughout the valley. We were told to place the hair samples into zip lock bags, take a picture of each body from which we had cut the hair using a digital camera, then label each bag of hair with the corresponding photo name.

My medic and I looked at each other in disbelief, and we set out on foot with a few Kurds towards the north side of Sargat to get the job done. I immediately arrived at the edge of a seemingly endless expanse of dead and disfigured human bodies.

The first dead person I encountered was severely burned. His lips were burnt off one side of the mouth along with most of his face. This created a horrifying snarl expression, because his teeth and burnt gums were exposed only on one side. The combination of the ghastly snarl, the burnt and wrinkled black eyes that seemed to peer through my soul, the smell of his burnt flesh, and the contorted frozen expression on his face seemed almost supernatural to me. I reached out and grabbed his hair, *touched his hair*, and snipped some off. I was so close to him I could see individual gnarled facial hairs protruding from the pores of his lifeless skin. His head wobbled a bit like an unstable inanimate object in a hideously abnormal way, unresponsive to my touch. I was sickened as I stuffed the hair into a plastic bag; almost forgot to breath as I stood over the corpse, and then I continued through the rolling hills of death before me that were littered with motionless mangled corpses. I think I confirmed the existence of Hell this day.

There was a group of 5 bodies that had been charred and melted together into a heap of gore; almost like a pile of slightly melted and burned human wax figures. The pile was mostly blackened, but also consisted of twisted skin and sizzled human fat, burnt clothing and equipment, and exposed and broken bones and entrails. One of the men's abdomen was burned through, so his intestines had spilled out and were also charred. The motionlessness of their bodies and eyes was indescribable. Their mouths were agape under empty eye sockets, or partial eyes, and they wore perpetual expressions of pain and agony. It was as if a demented artist had erected a monument to horror.

The level of anxiety I felt as I approached the pile made my entire body go so numb and tingly that I could barely feel myself.

One of the Kurds said the pile of men had been hit with a 106mm round; I guessed it was an incendiary round because that's the only thing that could have burned them to death so fast that they couldn't separate in time, hence causing the *merging via melting* that I stood there looking at in awe, shuddering. As I got close enough to cut some hair, the smell of burnt flesh was staggering as I inhaled their fumes. I cut some hair off the ones that actually still had small patches of hair left; crispy flesh fell off in some places because of the movement when I grabbed...touched...felt... the hair in order to cut it. I was careful not to pull too hard on the hair to extend it so I could cut it, because I didn't want to pull the partially encrusted scalp off with it, and if the hair was singed, I didn't want to break it. It was very difficult to force myself to touch them, and at one point I almost passed out from forgetting to breathe again.

Another had blown himself up with a suicide bomb vest. Some of the AAI had strapped themselves with explosives so they could blow us up if we overran them during the battle. This guy was one example and he'd blown himself in half. Entrails, dark red, with small clumps of dirt stuck to them, mangled and slightly burned, were hanging out of his lower torso and broken twisted legs. So much blood had drained from this half of his body that there was a coagulated trail of sticky darkness extending probably 50 feet down the sloped we were standing on. It was a seemingly impossible amount of blood; surreal. The body smelled like feces because of the exploded and exposed intestines dangling out of the torso. The whole area actually smelled like feces because of the scattered pieces of intestines that were spread around the area from the blast.

Some of his upper shoulders and head, attached to broken, shredded, and burned arms with bones extruding in fragments from them, were about 20 feet uphill. One side of his ribcage was ripped open and presented itself like some kind of monster's claw, draped in shredded meat. The face, mouth gaping and impossibly crooked, with dead eyes facing different directions, was perverted into a bizarre unnatural expression, and the horrifyingly demented position of the head evinced a brutally broken neck. He had those same relentless eyes...and the motionlessness really got to me again. He still had some good hair, so I kneeled down, grabbed some and cut it. It's impossible to convey or describe the emotion elicited by being inches away from, and touching, mutilated dead human bodies like this. Horror is the only word that comes to mind, but that word still fails to deliver the magnitude of the sentiment that overcame me– sheer dreadfulness, sheer anguish, and other wordless emotions, overcame my soul.

Another brutalized corpse was smashed into a small aqueduct that ran laterally across the ridge. His face was completely concave like a bowl; pushed inward all the way back to the *back of the inside* of his skull, similar to how a deflated soccer ball can be pushed into itself. This made his eyes bizarrely face each other, and stare past each other. Brains, grey and chunky, and a large pool of black coagulated blood were splattered underneath the broken and twisted neck, and upper body. I tried to imagine how this could have happened but could not completely figure it out.[25] I bent down, put my left knee on the ground, then swung my right leg over his body onto the other side of the small aqueduct, hence straddling the carcass. I looked deeply into his frozen concave and sparsely bearded face, and into those open but empty eyes. I drew a shuddering breath as I mustered up the courage to reach down closer to cut off some of his hair. It was difficult to cut, because it was like most of the hair was inside of a bowl. I pulled the hair pretty hard to detach the skin from the skull slightly so I could get the scissors inside the bowl enough to cut off a decent amount from the area above his forehead. It made a sickening wet ripping sound as I pulled the skin from the skull. I cut the hair, then I slipped as I was getting up from the straddle position with the hair in one hand and scissors in the other, and I got some blood and brains on my hand as well as my fingerless black leather gloves.

One body was still bleeding somehow, very slowly. A Kurd standing over the corpse explained that this bleeding AAI man had killed his brother during the attack. The Kurd poked the body with his barrel, holding the AK by the pistol grip. The way he poked the body was as if he was simply poking a piece of meat and he did it with no expression on his face or any indication of emotion whatsoever. This is when I fully understood how numb the Peshmerga are to the brutality of war. I cut the hair and kept moving forward, wading through the filth.

We cut hair and took pictures most of the day, switching places at times. The images are all still vivid in my mind. A head that had been savagely ripped off was on the ground with no sign of a body anywhere near it, a seemingly impossible scenario; we cut its hair. A body was blown in half the long way from crotch to neck, peeled apart into a heart shape with the head in the middle; we cut the hair. Legs on the ground. Arms on the ground. Fingers. Feet. Hands. Sections of spinal columns. Meaty ribcages. Skull shards with patches of hair. Fragments of bone and skin and randomly distributed chunks of muscle meat. The smell of burnt hair and flesh and feces and gunpowder permeated the air. Everywhere I looked across the expanse before me, hundreds of yards in any direction, a view of something awful could not be escaped. Death was maddeningly and inescapably *everywhere* and literally made my head spin. [26]

Finally, we ran out of plastic bags, so we silently walked back through Hell holding dozens of zip lock bags full of hair samples and a digital camera, down to the house we had stayed the night in. We hadn't even put a dent in the amount of dead bodies there were in terms of collecting hair samples, but at least it was over.

Imagine looking across 100 football fields and seeing a mangled dead body or cluster of dead bodies lying every five yards across the entire expanse. It was like a scene out of some absurd zombie apocalypse movie. The Kurds were throwing bodies into trucks like cordwood towards the end of the day. I was stunned at how mechanically they did it. They had to get the bodies out of there somehow since Kurdish families were already moving into houses in Sargat, and to do it effectively they just had to stop feeling anything. The Kurds have spent generations in war; they had it down to a science.

We found passports from countries all over the world on the dead bodies and in the buildings in Sargat. They hailed from multiple North African countries, Iran, Syria, Saudi Arabia, Lebanon, Turkey, Afghanistan, and there was even a member of the PLO there from Palestine, and that's just a few.[27]

The notion of achieving glory on the field of battle, which I had dreamt of my entire adult life, was crushed. I was immensely sick and exhausted, traumatized, and thoroughly disgusted with the whole scene, including my own performance during the battle (since I had frozen). The only thing that helped me cope was that we had just made more room for the Kurds to live in peace (as much as they ever could I guess), and we got rid of a bunch of psychos in this corner of Iraq. I kept telling myself this over and over to rationalize what I'd just experienced.

We spent another day in the Halabja area, firing rockets and mortars at members of AAI as they escaped into Iran. The sound of the Katooshas and mortars became maddening; every time one fired all the fibers in my body tensed and tore. I watched many dozens of AAI in the distance climbing over the snow packed peaks along the border on foot; black specs moved across the white peaks that pointed high into the huge blue sky over Iran. Periodically, the Iranian border positions also fired at them as they tried to get into Iran. Because of the immense terrain, most of them got away.

As I watched so many AAI fighters escape into the mountains, I felt surprised, and then disappointed in the reality that we hadn't actually killed *all* of them. Did we succeed? Then I thought about where they'd pop up next and whether what we had just done had been pointless or not. If there had been approximately one thousand AAI, and we'd killed about 300 of them, then where did the rest of them go and what would they do next? How many had already fled days or weeks before the impending attack, and where did they go? I didn't have time or energy to deeply contemplate these questions. We eventually said goodbye to the PUK in Halabja; they said we fought like tigers, but I didn't feel like a tiger. We drove to the Kurdish Headquarters at ASW to receive our next mission.[28]

My quest had finally brought me to a real war, but that didn't mean it was over. We prepared to head out towards the Green Line to take on the Iraqi Army.

Chapter 4
The Green Line
Tuz, Iraq

After Viking Hammer I drove to the PUK Peshmerga headquarters near the As Sulaymaniyah airstrip, where we had lived during most of the AFO mission; it had become the Headquarters for my Battalion, the 3Rd Battalion 10th Special Forces Group, and the war was in full motion. I was overwhelmed by the energy and dynamism at the headquarters as I watched thousands of Peshmerga rushing around as we drove through the gate. I acquired a fresh supply of ammunition and we received new Land Rovers; the four door Defender model.

We stayed for a few hours, and I quickly ate some baklava and caught up with one of my German speaking Peshmerga friends. My team leadership was given new orders, and soon we departed for our Company Headquarters, which I was told was located on the north side of the village of Cham Chamal.

After a short drive south, we arrived at my Company headquarters to find that it was only slightly more advanced than a shack. It was a dilapidated concrete block building that was nestled into the north side of a steep ridge, very well protected from any potential Iraqi rocket or mortar fire from the Green Line. My company commander, the same very calm and collected intellectual who led our infiltration into Iraq for the AFO mission, met us out front waving and looking positive. We all shook his hand with a smile and he told us what a great job we'd done against AAI. Then he brought us inside the concrete shack to tell us what we needed to do.

We stood in a semi-circle in a dingy and dimly lit little room facing a map that was clumsily taped to the peeling wall. I could smell our collective body odor since we hadn't taken a shower in about two weeks, and I still didn't feel well. My team's mission was to go south into the unknown and somehow locate and link up with an element of about 5000 randomly dispersed Peshmerga, then conduct bombing and harassing missions against the two tank brigades of Iraqi military (after figuring out where they were), and then eventually attack the city of Tuz. He pointed to a massive area east of Kirkuk and north of Tuz on the huge map. He told us that while we operated in the Tuz area, the rest of the company was going to seize Kirkuk with about twenty thousand Peshmerga.[29]

He also told us that some conventional Airborne unit had flown through ultra-secure airspace and parachuted into a massively secure Airstrip up in the Kurdish KDP sector somewhere, and we all wondered why they hadn't just landed on the airstrip. We assumed they were just trying to be cool.

My commander reminded us that the whole reason for the Task Force Viking northern front was to harass the Iraqi Army enough so they would not go south to fight against our main attack force that was headed for Baghdad. I wondered why we didn't take all the Kurds into Baghdad to become the main effort *ourselves*, rather than the conventional forces. We made a quick plan, our commander wished us luck, and we headed southeast.

I had no idea where we were going, other than we were going to an area north of Tuz, to drive around with the hope of eventually finding some friendly Kurds prior to bumping into thousands of Iraqi troops. As we rolled down the road away from the shack and towards the Green Line, my company commander faded in the distance behind us. Yet again, I was relentlessly driving forward towards uncertainty, this time towards the Iraqi front line.

The road that shot south-eastward from Cham Chamal was awful. We named it "the road of doom" after we hit a dip in the road that literally sent us airborne. I saw several goat herders along the way, and they waved and smiled. The terrain in this area was quite different than up in the mountains deep inside Kurdistan. Very little grass was present, what little I did see was brown. There were wadis with flat stones and light brown sandy dirt, and it looked like what I expected to see on the outskirts of a desert. We drove very nervously for several hours, we didn't know if we could trust anyone, so we were careful not to rush up on strangers who were also driving on the roads. It was entirely possible to me that around every corner we might run right into an entire thousands-strong Iraqi Army unit, because I really didn't know where anything was. Finally, after a few very tenuous hours, I saw a line of vehicles up ahead that looked like Peshmerga.

We drove past the line of vehicles, I was ready for a gunfight at any moment, until finally we arrived at a small cluster of reddish clay buildings, and there were some Peshmerga standing around. When we pulled up, about fifty Peshmerga came out of the huts and met us with smiles; I immediately felt more secure (not all Kurds could automatically be considered friendly, there were many factions of Kurds). My team sergeant and Captain got out with our interpreter and talked to them for a bit. Everyone seemed positive, and apparently, they told my leadership where we needed to go to centralize ourselves in respect to how the Peshmerga were generally distributed across our enormous area of responsibility. We took off again and followed a few random Peshmerga vehicles.

Finally, after driving though windy roads past hundreds of abandoned Iraqi bunkers and positions, over militarized hilltops covered in razor wire and interlocking trenches, and straddling some tank mines that were dug into the road, we reached an area where there was a small rectangular one-story building on the left side. It had a flat roof, and in the area behind the building there were large amounts of pipes and pumps that covered about a 200 meter square area, which made a crude foreground to an endless expanse of desolate, flat, dry terrain under a massive blue sky. There was also another building in the same area, about one hundred meters to our left. It was also white, low, and concrete block with a few windows. The immediate surroundings were largely rock, sand, and randomly dispersed tufts of brownish grass. I was afraid that every building we saw might have been some kind of chemical weapons depot for WMD. Part of me hoped we'd be the ones who found the smoking gun.[30] This building would be our new home for a while, so we set up our satellite radio communications and established a security plan. Within minutes, we discovered Peshmerga had occupied the other building, and they came over with tea.

The Peshmerga explained the situation to a few of us, and what they'd been doing. They had spread out into dozens, possibly hundreds, of tiny teams, and they were conducting mortar and harassing attacks against the Iraqi Army on the outskirts of both Tuz and Kirkuk (and ultimately across the entire Green Line). They were using the wadis and the terrain to get close the Iraqi front line. They were excited to see us start calling in air strikes on the highly vulnerable Iraqi units they had observed. The Peshmerga told us the Iraqi military had occupied a large ridge just northeast of Tuz, and they were dug in all along the road that led northwest from Tuz to Kirkuk. It was our responsibility to kill them.

After a sleepless night, the next day we began operations. We had a very simple job: go find the Iraqi Military, bring some Kurds for security, and call in air strikes. My whole team was devastatingly tired, so only two of us at a time went out to the observation points (OPs) that the Kurds had already established. We slept only a short distance from the front line of tens of thousands of Iraqi troops, and it only took a half hour or less, moving over rough terrain, to get close enough to see hundreds of them with the naked eye. I developed a permanent eerie feeling when I looked at the map and realized that tens of thousands of enemy troops were right up the road, and we didn't have dedicated air support and only a handful of anti-tank weapons. They could have dropped artillery on us or overran us easily if they'd known where we were; I actually wondered why they didn't just attack us.

On my first patrol out to the Green Line, to attack the Iraqi units, I drove with the Kurds in their vehicles. I jumped up and smiled to them all as I crammed myself into the back of a pickup between a few smelly Peshmerga who had dirty faces, dark suntans, and they were constantly grinning at me from under their black and white headwraps. One of them pointed up in the air and kept smiling and saying "siarra, siarra." I didn't know what that meant, until he reached out and grabbed the antenna that stuck out of my radio pouch and pointed at the sky again, and made some bomb dropping and explosion sounds. Siarra meant "aircraft," and they were very excited to see what American aircraft could do. They would not be disappointed.

I thought to myself, "here I go again," as I bounced down a dusty dirt road, moving forward in the back of a primitive truck full of smiling Kurds, headed towards the enemy and the unknown. The trucks slowed down after a few dusty and bumpy minutes, and the Kurds chattered quietly and restlessly. I dismounted with a clatter, and I continued on foot in a southerly direction surrounded by the small team of Peshmerga, towards the Iraqi front line, concealed within the low, sandy, and dry wadi floor. We rounded many corners and traversed a few small knolls. I was getting very close to the ridgeline that was just to the north of Tuz, where hundreds, maybe thousands of enemy Iraqi soldiers were.

The Kurds chattered to each other and pointed upwards, then started climbing up a small hill to my left front. As they got to the top they began crawling so they wouldn't silhouette themselves. I took out my spotting scope from my small pack, and followed them up. I was also with one other Green Beret from my team as well and our Air Force Special Tactics (STS) guy. I stayed low and crawled into place next to the Peshmerga. I laid in the prone position and looked south towards the massive tan and blue expanse of the Green Line. The view was alarming.

Without even using the high powered spotting scope, I observed Iraqi Army positions for as far left and right as my eyes were capable of perceiving. The "enemy" was sprawled in front of me for literally as far as I could see; as if they constituted the actual horizon. There were trucks, antennae, buildings, cars, hundreds of soldiers walking around, bunkers, uniformed Iraqi soldiers standing in formation, and far to my right-front there was a road with some military vehicles driving up and down it. I was about 1000 meters away, which felt very close in this open terrain. From the distance, the scene looked like a military

91

version of a giant ant farm under an endless desert sky; I felt tiny in contrast. I started looking at specifics through the spotting scope.

I focused the scope on an individual soldier who was half exposed, standing in what appeared to be a foxhole, quite a distance away from the rest of his unit – closer to us. His movements indicated a bit of boredom and misery to me. I could almost see his facial expressions through the spotting scope, and he was easily visible with the naked eye. When I was an infantryman, I had been in similar situations to his (before I joined the Green Berets), except in my experience it was just training. I thought about how oppressive it was to stand in a foxhole for days or weeks on end, and I was quite sure that it's a completely different, and a much worse experience, when you are waiting for the United States Air Force to drop bombs on you. A feeling of empathy for him swept over me, and the sheer presence of this feeling surprised me. His green helmet casted a shadow over half of his young, tan face, and I think he was talking to himself. I used to talk to myself when I was in a foxhole too.

Our STS guy called for AWACS on the radio, and within the hour a jet was "inbound" for our usage. As the aircraft approached, the Kurds started to get very excited, and the Iraqis started to scurry before me as the seemingly omnipresent crackling noise in the sky increased. It looked like someone had tapped on the ant farm's glass, or shaken it. That lone soldier ducked down into his foxhole and disappeared below the surface, all that was left was a tiny dark hole in the brown earth. I took note that there were still dozens of soldiers on the road in front of a cliff along the ridge in front of Tuz when the bombs hit.[31]

Boom, Boom, Boom....

The concussions from the bombs were unimaginably vicious; the bombs must have been bigger than the ones we used on Viking Hammer. They produced god-like cracks of thunder that shook the earth; shock waves permeated my intestines and skull even though I was 1000 meters away. Massive amounts of dust, flame, and black smoke curled hundreds of feet into the big sky like nebulous skyscrapers. I thought deeply for a second about what it must be like to be one of those tiny Iraqis down there; the horror. The noise from the blasts dissipated into the distance while I watched a terrible scene unfold through a gap in the dust and smoke.

A large chunk of the north side of the cliff above where the Iraqis were standing on the road collapsed from the blast. Through my spotting scope I watched clearly as a huge avalanche of rock and sand buried at least a dozen of the soldiers alive; they made futile attempts to escape their fate, but they were overcome in an instant. I forgot to breathe for so long that blackness swept into my vision as my oxygen depleted, and I almost passed out. I actually forgot to breathe. Every muscle in my body became so tense that my jaw cramped and muscle spasms rippled through my thighs and trapezoids. As the wind blew the black clouds that still hung over the Iraqis to my left and dissipated, my tunnel vision faded as I regained my ability to breath. I hoped my teammates didn't notice my response to what just happened, because they didn't seem to be as bothered. I then noticed there were dozens of dark human forms laying on the ground around where each of the bombs had hit; motionless, dead.

Through the spotting scope I could almost see the burnt faces of the dead, and of course after the haircutting episode in Sargat I had plenty of material for my imagination to generate a clear picture of what those dead and mutilated Iraqi soldiers looked like down there.

While we waited for more aircraft for another several hours, the Iraqis meandered around, and I assumed they were trying to figure out what to do with the dead people. They started consolidating the dead as we decided to return to our compound. Just before I crawled backwards off the hill, I focused my scope on that one lone Iraqi's foxhole. He stood back up and adjusted his green helmet, then continued to talk to himself. Something about seeing him alive made me feel better, but I didn't know what it was. I was confused by why I had so much sympathy for him, and why seeing him alive made me feel better (and I felt guilty because it made me feel better). As a soldier, was it ok for me to feel *anything*?

We continued to operate like this for several weeks, which seemed like an eternity. We basically ran shifts, and continuously bombed the Iraqis with immeasurable brutality. I didn't like the fact that the Iraqi soldiers were not attacking us and didn't really seem to pose much of a threat, yet we were still doing our job and killing them. On one occasion they fired some artillery at us, and that brought back that old helpless doom feeling I was now very familiar with, but that didn't help me get over the fact that they were always just sitting there out in the open, powerless against our aircraft, facing imminent death. I felt like a kid standing in front of an ant farm with a giant magnifying glass.

One night, over tea, as we talked about the day's events with the Kurds, they told us that the Iraqi military officer leadership was actually killing their own soldiers because some of the soldiers were trying to run away to escape inevitable death. If this information was true, we were bombing Iraqi soldiers who were being forced by their officer leadership to sit there and die. Moreover, by proxy, the officers were forcing themselves to die as well. It didn't make any sense to me. My years old notion that war would be glorious further faded in my conscience.

One time while I was out on an OP, I heard small arms fire from where the Iraqis were, and I imagined that the shots fired were from Iraqi officers killing their men for trying to leave. From that point on, when I was on an OP, I stopped watching the bombs drop. Something in my mind and conscience had changed; It was hard to see the bombs hit people anymore. I looked away or put my head down after we told the pilots "you're cleared hot." I was growing detached and numb, and I grew very disappointed in myself for thinking and questioning these things.[32]

I kept my thoughts a secret until my Captain and I had a conversation late one night. He introduced me to the notion that it would be better if we dropped leaflets to encourage the Iraqi soldiers to surrender, rather than dropping bombs on them. I was glad I wasn't the only one feeling like what we were doing was not optimal. If we kept killing all the soldiers, then who would become the new Iraqi security forces when the war was over? If we bombed them like this for much longer, would we drive them into the arms of the local terrorist groups? Would they join a reconstituted Ansar Al Islam? Why were we doing this and what was the strategy behind it? We talked about it for a long time that night, and several times after; we cared enough about this idea to propose it to our headquarters.[33]

I threw stones when I was back on radio duty, which made me think of the time I pitched a no-hitter in the Connecticut shoreline baseball championships when I was a kid, and I thought about my family a lot. Many days passed. I read the intelligence summaries (INTSUMs) and situation reports (SITREPs) every day. The SITREP was useful because it told us what everyone else was doing in the war, but the INTSUMs were high level and mostly useless to our operations; our Peshmerga comrades provided much more specific and useful information. We had tea with the Kurds and let them shoot our weapons for fun. We traded stories about the different ways we'd seen Iraqis die along the Green Line. One day our old CIA team buddies showed up we swapped a few war stories with them.

We dug a slit trench in the side yard, and the smell from it somehow attracted a pack of dogs. The dogs frequently ate our feces. One of the guys on my team named each dog, and we assigned the dogs the collective title of "The Turd Burglars." Some of the dogs were vicious, and they often barked all night. Grit, who had no patience for such things, shot and killed a few of the dogs for barking too much. I didn't mind the barking, because I couldn't sleep anyway.

During one random conversation, one of the guys on my team suggested that maybe we could just drive right into the Iraqi units' area and try to get them to surrender. He was joking, but after my experiences in Bosnia and Kosovo, I actually think that his idea was not far from an invalid thought. I started to understand what my father meant when he said he always wanted to just go shake the Vietcong's hands because he was sure they could have all just gotten along ok.

One day I called home on a satellite phone. I talked to my father in Connecticut from out in front of our building in Iraq. I told him that everything was ok. He told me to *never think anything is ok during a war* and to not get complacent. It was damn good advice from a Silver Star recipient with three purple hearts and four major bullet injuries (Vietnam). He also told me my wife and daughter were doing ok living with them, but my mom's hair was falling out and my wife had lost almost 20 pounds from the stress of wondering where I was within the craziness they were watching on the news. The news had reported a friendly fire incident involving the Kurds and Special Forces, and they thought it could have been me, and had no easy way to confirm or deny. I hated the stress I was putting them through, and I hoped that I would survive to see them all again.

On one particular rotation out to an OP, I encountered two truckloads of Kurds waiting on the side of the road. I was always very jovial and super friendly to the Kurds, because I genuinely liked and trusted them and I wanted to always keep a good rapport, so I asked them if they wanted to come with me. They were all smiles, and with a rattle of weapons and equipment, they loaded up and followed us down the wadis.

We navigated in vehicles for a while, then on foot through the wadis until we were very close to the Iraqis and arrived at a place near the road that led from Tuz to Kirkuk. We got in position and started spotting for targets.

The Air Force STS guy got AWACS on the radio, and we waited. The Kurds made tea behind some cover, and when they were done they asked us when the aircraft would arrive. They were surprised when I told them that we don't have aircraft dedicated to us, we only got leftovers. I laughed when they told us that they thought every single one of us had our own *personal* siarra. Then something new happened.

I saw several Iraqi tanks maneuvering, and it looked like they were headed our way.

You have not felt fear until you've seen a military *tank*, an *enemy* tank, moving towards you. A tank is a giant machine that is completely engineered for the sole purpose of war and ultimately the administration of human death. When I saw the tanks, it was equivalent to seeing the grim reaper, and the presence of such evil evoked a familiar, but still immeasurable feeling of doom. My blood ran cold and my nerves almost burst with tingling electricity when I also noticed dozens of large Iraqi 2.5 ton personnel trucks, more tanks, and hundreds of bustling Iraqi soldiers. The Kurds started chattering nervously. When the Kurds got nervous, I got *really* nervous. The STS guy miraculously got an aircraft on call, which was as refreshing to know as it was to finally see the Iraqis become an actual threat.

I overheard the radio as I laid next to the STS guy, and I could hear the pilot talking. Not only were there Iraqi tanks driving around in front of us, there were also many tanks dug into the ground. The jet pilot told us he was going to use a technique called "high angle strafe." "High angle strafe" is when the pilot soars straight up in the air over the target, then drops straight down nose first and fires the chain guns onto the top of their prey. Buried tanks, also called "revetted," are not vulnerable to indirect surface blasts, but their tops are completely exposed to high angle strafe.

The pilot flew with an almost sinister form of elegance, far up into the massive sky until the aircraft became a silver spec on what looked like the edge of the troposphere. The aircraft seemingly hovered for an instant, and then slowly and gracefully fell into a nose-dive. Violent bursts from the main gun completely pummeled the revetted tanks and the ground around them. Each round produced three sounds in rapid succession; the bark of the shot, the streaming of the round towards the ground, then the thud of when the round hit the target. These three sounds happened at the rate of thousands of rounds per minute, which produced violence at imperceptible scale. The roar of the main gun provided foreground for the immense sound of the jet ripping the giant Iraqi sky in half. The plane's methodical up and down movements reminded me of a music conductor's hand, but instead of music there was the sound of jet engines mixed with the burp of the machine gun, and the result was death rather than a melody.

After the aircraft had finished its relentless strafing runs and ran out of ammunition, dozens of tendrils of black smoke rose from the scorched kill zone. The wind moved the slender swaying tendrils to my left in unison, and they looked like hundreds of giant morphing apparitions as the wind changed their shapes, until they finally dissipated at random across the massive landscape. There were still thousands of Iraqi soldiers out there in front of me as we packed up and walked away. The thought that these tanks and trucks were maneuvering on us again made me feel better. Because if they had been, that meant the Iraqis were trying to fight us, and that made me feel less guilty about the previous weeks of slaughter.

When I got back to the refinery, I immediately discovered that the Iraqis had not been maneuvering on us. They were preparing to move south out of the area. I was disappointed but didn't have time to contemplate. My Captain said we were going to attack and occupy Tuz immediately, *that very minute*, with about three thousand Peshmerga. The rest of my company was already on the move to seize Kirkuk with another massive Peshmerga horde.

In less than ten minutes we were packed and ready to go. I was the driver that night. I did not look forward to driving, especially since it was growing dark, and my eyes caused me even more trouble at night than they did normally. I took a deep breath, grasped the steering wheel tightly, depressed the accelerator, and my vehicle lurched forward towards Tuz and yet another unknown set of dangerous circumstances. Within a few minutes it became pitch dark, and we encountered a large convoy of random vehicles full of Peshmerga along the road.

They had 2.5 ton green trucks, jeeps, land rovers, motorcycles, and some had cars or taxi cabs; the scene was quite similar to the assembly of Peshmerga for Operation Viking Hammer. I drove behind my Captain's Land Rover, past dozens of vehicles and cheering Kurds, and he was behind a Kurdish 2.5 ton truck. Some Kurdish trucks joined our convoy, and I drove with them for about a half an hour in the same general direction as usual.

For several hours, I followed blurry rear headlights in the blackness and watched the ambient light barely penetrate the darkness and bounce off fractals of stone and sand in my peripheral vision. I felt like I was on an expedition through the dark side of the moon. We moved along rocky wadis and then through extremely rough terrain that I definitely hadn't been through before. I had no idea where we were, and soon I heard weapons fire popping in the distance. The weapons fire quickly grew from sporadic to continuous as we grew closer to the outskirts of Tuz. I reached the top of a rise that provided a vantage point over the road that led from Kirkuk into Tuz.

On the road below me about a kilometer to my right, I saw hundreds of Iraqi military vehicles on the dark road with their headlights on for as far as I could see. The lights were backdropped by complete darkness, so the meandering line of lights looked like a giant miles-long snake floating in deep space. The road looked like it was completely packed all the way from Tuz to Kirkuk. The Iraqis were definitely leaving Kirkuk and Tuz, and it looked like *all of them*. We pressed forward, and I thought we'd be in a serious battle with the Iraqis in a few minutes. However, just as I left that vantage point, something unforgettable happened.

The Kurdish truck in front of us was suddenly hit by an explosion.

We were in a minefield.

Everyone stopped, the truck in front of us was smoking, and the front of it was mangled. The Peshmerga instantly began yelling frantically. My mind went wild with fear, and my heart pounded as my body became overrun with tension and stress like I'd been hit with a stun gun. The Kurds walked around with flashlights, jabbering incessantly in urgent pitched voices. White light from Kurds with flashlights danced across the rocky and sandy terrain and their voices grew more and more intense. They found mines everywhere. They even found many mines *behind us*, which meant we'd been lucky we made it as far as we had. This also meant there was no turning back; it was just as dangerous to go back as it was to go forward, and because of the terrain, and the darkness of the night, it would have been impossible to perfectly retrace our steps.

The Kurds asked us if we had anything that they could use to mark the mines. Luckily, we had several boxes of mini chemlights, so we passed them out. The Kurds, and some of my teammates, got out of the land rovers, very carefully, and started marking the mines (that they could find) using flashlights to carefully place chemlights next to each mine. The plan was to drive forward and straddle the chemlights and everyone would stay in line. There was nothing else we could do.

It was pitch black. My eyes contorted the glow of the chemlights terribly. The feeling of doom I previously felt from tanks and from being pinned down by machine gun fire was nothing compared to the spirit-crushing feeling that hit me as I released the clutch, depressed the gas, and continued onward through the minefield. Thinking became pointless after a few minutes, and I expected to be ripped to shreds at every moment as I straddled the blurry chemlights. I continuously squinted my eyes in a futile attempt to make the chemlights clearer, and hoped like hell that if I did run over a mine that it would at least kill me instantly and not leave me mangled. I had no idea how far we had to go to reach the end of this minefield, and there was no guarantee that we had marked all the mines; I expected to become red mist at every nanosecond, and the feeling of stress was unimaginable. I could not imagine anything less glorious than being killed by a landmine.

I drove like this *all night*. My jaw began to ache, and I realized it was because I had been clenching my teeth in anticipation of being blown up for so many hours. When we ran out of chem lights, the Kurds started reusing the ones from behind us. Eventually, hours later we made it out of the minefield and into the outskirts of Tuz. I was glad when we reached pavement. We moved through an area where we were surrounded by a large volume of weapons fire. The Kurds said that the fighting was *not Kurds against the Iraqis*. I didn't understand. If it wasn't the Kurds fighting the Iraqis, then who was fighting who?

We eventually made it to an actual road. I was too tired and emotionally bludgeoned to feel relieved that we were out of the minefield. It was still dark, and we pulled into someone's house in Tuz. A very friendly Kurd invited us into his house, led us into a musty and dark room with low ceilings and concrete walls, and then gave us tea and bread. We were told we would hide there until the battles were over.

Early in the morning, way before daylight broke, when I was the only one awake, still painfully tense, a little Kurdish girl, probably 4 or 5 years old, came to the doorway of her living room in a simple tan sleeping dress, where my team was sleeping amongst our piles of kit. When I turned my weary head to look at her tiny form standing in the doorway, she just stood there in the dim light and stared at me with big and curious dark eyes. Her face wore a surprisingly intense expression that I oddly perceived as what appeared to be *hope*. I smiled big and gently waved my fingerless black gloved hand, trying to be as small and friendly looking as a dirty and unshaven, six foot three, 225 pound, traumatized, American Green Beret possibly could. She smiled back, gripped her dress anxiously, and her big dark eyes lit up with pure joy; simply because I turned out to be nice. She gave me a very shy and microscopic wave, and then she turned and dashed away down the hall and out of sight; seemingly delighted. I thought of my baby daughter, and I imagined she would have been just as curious and hopeful for niceness if there were suddenly a bunch of Peshmerga laying in *her* living room one night. That little girl gave me a burst of motivation, and I swore to myself again that I would make it out of Iraq alive to see my family. [34]

I slept for an hour at most, and at sunset my Captain and Grit went outside to figure out what to do next. They came back in with news that we were going to stay with a Peshmerga unit near the center of Tuz. We said goodbye to the owner of the house, I looked for the little girl to say goodbye, but I couldn't find her.

We left and drove down a paved road towards the center of Tuz. We passed blown up tanks and cars, and I watched Kurds scavenging material from everywhere and everything. Some people towed Anti-Aircraft guns with Taxi cabs, and others drove tanks. I kept staring numbly at the dead human beings laying in contorted positions, strewn about the sides of the road like trash. One body had been completely flattened like a bug, complete with guts squirting out, by a tank. As we drove towards the center of Tuz, I noticed that various groups of people had raised flags of all different types randomly throughout the city, and there were men with guns, *armed militants*, generally assembled around where each of the flags were. I didn't understand why there were so many groups.

I was tired as hell when we arrived at our new home, which was a compound of deteriorating buildings surrounded by a crude block wall about 5 feet high. When I looked around as one naturally does, I guessed the compound had been a school or a small Iraqi Army barracks. I unloaded my gear and established myself in a narrow one-story rectangular building with many empty window openings. The Kurdish leadership for the area came to our building and gave us an update on the situation.

They informed us that the siege of Kirkuk and Tuz were over. However, I was surprised when they told us that over 16 different militant, political, ethnic, and tribal groups had occupied Tuz, and they were all fighting for territory. This information explained all the different flags I'd seen flying as we drove in, as well as the fighting I had heard while driving through the minefield. Even the Islamic Group of Kurdistan (IGK) had secured a spot. [35]

The next day we decided to explore the ridge that we had repetitively bombed in the weeks prior to invading Tuz. We drove up to the top of the ridgeline, near where all those Iraqis had been buried in the avalanche. The terrain was like a rocky desert, like a wasteland, and there were Iraqi military uniforms and equipment strewn across the brown and reddish landscape for as far as I could see. I could see for miles to the north and northeast once we reached the top of the ridge. The terrain looked like a sea of sand and rock, and veins of wadis extended out to the horizon line. I peered northeastward, towards where we used to sit in the OPs to call air strikes. I realized as I perceived the enormous expanse below me, that it was no wonder the Iraqis could never see us; we would have been mere specks on this moonlike landscape. The most memorable aspect of exploring this thoroughly bombed ridge was when we approached what looked like a horse, or a donkey, I couldn't tell anymore.

The once-beautiful animal, a female, was laying on its side, barely alive. She had almost no skin left on the side of her body that was facing up, and the skin that was left was burned severely. Her eyes were burned almost completely out, and her ears were burnt off. What was left of her eyes was blackened and twisted, or had a hideous veil of what appeared to be burnt cornea. Her teeth were exposed as a snarl due to most of her lips having been burnt off in a similar way as the dead AAI fighter I had cut hair from a month prior. Although those things were horrific, the part that shocked and bothered me the most was the state of the poor animal's legs, which were hopelessly shredded. Each leg looked as if it had been flayed and the bone had been removed, and then the sheath of skin and muscle that should have surrounded the bone had been cut crudely *the long way* into ribbons, except these ribbons consisted of charred reddish meat, which gave the animal the appearance of some kind of demented monster. The poor thing kept trying to stand because our movement had scared her, she could probably smell and hear us but not see us. She kept flapping her brutalized legs, the shards slapped against the ground in a terrible way and made a sort of splat sound, and she was producing a dreadful version of a neigh due to her damaged face. Since I am basically an animal loving country boy at heart who grew up around eastern Connecticut farms, this visualization was vile and heartbreaking. The degree of sadness I felt for that completely innocent animal surprised me, a victim of war and perhaps one of our airstrikes. One of the guys on my team shot her in the head with his pistol to put her out of her misery.

Shortly after our arrival in Tuz, the US declared that hostilities were over. The war was over. In the Kurdish areas there was infinite rejoicing. When we went across the street to buy food, we encountered a barrage of statements from people like "We love George Bush!" and "Bush Good!" To the Kurds we were heroes. However, the Kurds also thought the idea that the war was suddenly "over" was downright silly.

Our command told us that since the war was now over, we had a new mission. Our new mission was to link up with the different factions within the vicinity of Tuz, and report what was going on in order to provide situational awareness. We switched from all-out war to a peacekeeping mission in one instant. The drastic and abrupt change in mission was actually quite logical, what else could we have done at this point?

The next day my Warrant Officer and I drove around the city of Tuz to perform our new mission, just the two of us along with an interpreter. I was reminded of my time as a Joint Commissioned Observer (JCO) in post-war Bosnia, driving around freely, and observing how the normal people, the innocent bystanders of war, went about their business trying to deal with the aftermath of the hell they had just experienced. Frustrated women swept out houses while kids played outside, and men spoke to each other emotionally in the streets. I imagined what it would be like to be in their shoes. Some people waved to us, some just watched us go by. There were many different flags everywhere, and there were many small compound-like clusters of buildings that were encapsulated by razor wire or makeshift chain-link fencing with armed men in front.

As we randomly patrolled the streets just to see the state of Tuz and to get a feel for what had materialized, I saw the flag of IGK along the dirty grey road in the distance up ahead. The flag was inside of a small fenced compound with armed and bearded fighters guarding it. Recall that IGK was a group that let us target Ansar Al Islam during our AFO mission, but we had also targeted *them*. We had killed over one hundred of them in their headquarters in Khurmal. Since the war was over, my Warrant Officer insisted we try to meet with them to see what they were up to.[36] It was as if one moment it was our job to kill them, and the next it was our job to chat over tea.

We stopped in front of the building, parked, and since they didn't shoot at us immediately, we got out of our SUV and approached their compound. When we stepped out of the land rover, wearing US ARMY uniforms, the facial expressions on the IGK guards became tense and confused. As we approached, I tried my best not to look confrontational, and the two IGK men chatted nervously with each other, but never took their dark eyes off of us. I knew they were trying to decide whether they were supposed to kill us or not, so my body tensed in preparation for a gunfight and I gripped Old Sarge in anticipation. We made it up to where the men stood (without them shooting at us), then asked them if we could speak to their leader. They looked at each other with confusion in their eyes, murmured to each other and shrugged, and one of them turned and walked inside.

Within a few seconds, a thin man with a very robust, dense, shiny, and exceptionally well-maintained black beard walked across the light colored and sun smattered dirt in front of the crude whitewash building to greet us. His AK was slung over his tan equipment, and he had very intense dark eyes that were so deep black they contrasted interestingly with the hue of his light skin. He reminded me, in his face, his clothing, and equipment, like all the dead AAI fighters I had cut hair from.

I instinctually extended my hand to him and smiled, and he returned a calm smile back and shook my hand robustly. He invited us to sit down on a small bench in the front of the building. He told someone behind him to bring us all some tea, and we began to talk. I really wasn't surprised that he acted friendly, most people are when you approach them in a non-threatening manner, my adventures over the long days and short years prior had taught me that.

We sat down on a small wooden bench and sipped our tea once it arrived. His first question was exactly what I expected.

"Why did the US bomb IGK in Khurmal?"

I told him the truth; the US bombed IGK because IGK had supported AAI. While the interpreter translated it to the IGK leader I mentally prepared myself for a major gunfight. However, the IGK leader's expression became one of curiosity, and he seemed to think that what I said was a valid explanation. He proceeded to explain that his group was not like AAI, and they had not supported them. Essentially, after a few minutes of him trying to convince us that they were not evil and had not supported AAI, I realized he was just trying to convince us to leave his group alone. Basically, he was passively promising me that they were not a threat, and never would be, probably so we'd think there was no more reason to kill a bunch of them again. Regardless, IGK made some good tea, it tasted a little different than the Kurdish style I was used to. In the back of my mind I kept hoping that the tea was not poisoned as I sipped it. We left on a good note, and I didn't think they'd attack us.[37]

Over the next few weeks, we visited four different Turkmen groups, communist Kurd groups that were not PUK, and several Arab tribal groups to the west of Tuz. The Arab tribes were interesting to meet. One day I visited a particular tribe that lived in an area that I believe was west of the Tuz airstrip.

I drove west for a couple hours before I pulled up the main road of a desert village that was lined with primitive block and clay dwellings; all very bright with surface reflectance from the harsh sun. The road was bumpy, sandy white, and dusty. We stopped on the right side and got out of the SUV. We met some of the tribal leader's sons in the road. They were cordial and brought us up some stairs on the side of a whitewash house, into a large room, and we all sat cross legged on a carpet on the concrete floor. The room was dimly lit and smelled of tea. A very old man with a white beard, who was more wrinkled than any person I had ever witnessed in my life, constantly did laps around the room in a squatted position, wearing nothing but what amounted to a white loin cloth to cover his frail frame. He had a tea pot in his hand, and he constantly filled tea for everyone. I noticed he had really intense eyes and really gnarly toes when I thanked him for pouring my tea.

I surveyed the half dozen armed men who sat around the edge of the room, facing inwards, legs crossed, with their weapons on the floor beside them. Some of these young men looked deeply into my eyes with earnest, some looked me up and down with curiosity, and some were smiling and nodding their heads as if they wanted to say something but knew I wouldn't have understood their language. I felt an aura of antiquity and wisdom when the leader entered the room and the other men sat up straighter in response, which prompted me to take this situation very seriously. The leader of this group was very old and wrinkled, he sat sternly at the head of the rectangular room, and within a few minutes of casual conversation, he began to ask us about democracy. Our interpreter was terrified.

He asked how democracy worked. I explained the whole concept of voting and everything as best I could, the way it is done in America. He had a hard time understanding, and did not like, the logic of "the majority rules." It didn't make sense to him because if his tribe was simply smaller in numbers than any other tribe, then his tribe would inevitably lose in any election, and their interests would not be represented. We talked about it for a while and concluded that he had raised a great point. I wasn't in a position where it made sense to try and be overly persuasive. In tribal society, it's very difficult to drop democracy into the mix. He explained that the nature of tribes is high independence, homogeneity, and autonomy, and democracy *across* tribes poses a serious challenge, especially when religious and ethnic dynamics are also in play. He was concerned that without Sadaam keeping the tribes from fighting by ruling with an iron fist, the tribes would digress into complete chaos and warfare over territory and resources. I eventually left on a friendly note after shaking everyone's hands and thanking them all for the hospitality.

During our stay in Tuz, we had a bit more time on our hands than we had the weeks prior. The Kurds installed an interesting gravity fed outdoor shower for us, and we taught them how to play baseball in the open dirt area inside our small compound. We made massive trash bonfires in the center of the parking area in front of our building. I wrote poems and random stories on whatever paper I could find, and I asked the Kurds if they could find me a guitar anywhere, but they couldn't.

After about two weeks, I became sick with a brutal stomach infection. It was so bad my team medic was on the verge of calling a helicopter medevac for me. I was completely incapacitated for about four days. The only thing I was capable of doing was laying in the fetal position next to the filthy hole in the floor bathroom stall as large foreign insects crawled on me, repetitively vomiting and enduring incredible surges in pain from what my medic called "massive fluid shifts" in my intestines. I faded in and out of sleep, while I had terrible nightmares about the months and weeks prior. If we had been attacked, I don't think I would have been able to fight, that's how sick I was. He gave me two Z-Packs, and I eventually recovered. We also did something kind of strange.

Back in Colorado Springs, there was a great little restaurant called "The Western Omelet" that served the hottest and best tasting green chili in the world. We used to order omelets smothered in this green splendor after our grueling morning exercises. We all missed this place very badly and grew quite wistful about it. In fact, talking about it became sort of a hobby for us once we had all returned back to base from our daily patrols. One of the guys on my team, who had been a philosophy major in college, decided we should send the restaurant a picture of our team, accompanied by a very nostalgic and elaborately written note. So, we drove out and found a destroyed Iraqi tank along the road to Kirkuk somewhere and we posed for a picture. We stenciled a chili pepper onto the tank first using spray paint and a stencil made out of a piece of cardboard, and we also spray-painted "Western Omelet or Bust!" on the tank. We then wrote the letter and printed it along with the picture using our tiny printer we'd been carrying all the while. We asked one of our B-Team guys to figure out the address for us.[38]

The Kurds started to get randomly attacked by various militant groups. The attacks were from mostly Arab groups of different kinds, but some instances of chaos supposedly came from Turkmen groups. We thought this Turkmen problem was interesting, so my Warrant Officer and I again decided to see what some of these Turkmen groups were up to.

There were four different splinter groups of Turkmen in town, each had their own compound full of armed fighters. We drove up to the front of one of them at random, parked, and walked right up to the front gate. We smiled and shook hands with the several armed men who were guarding the place, and I asked if we could talk to whoever was in charge. They looked at each other, obviously confused a bit by our level of comfort, shrugged and said OK. They led us through a crowd of dozens of chattering armed men who wore different styles of headgear and clothing, all of which were staring at me inquisitively; I was nervous, but it didn't look like anyone was going to pull a trigger. We continued through a small gate, down a sidewalk, and into a typical concrete building. Inside the building It was quite dark, until we rounded a corner into an area that was better lit, and that's when I saw something interesting.

At first, I thought someone from my own Green Beret unit was standing there in front of us. This guy was in obviously good shape, and had what looked like an M4 carbine rifle (the same we used), with a large and interesting scope on it, along with an infrared aiming device of some kind, and a pistol grip under the front handguard. He also had a very fancy and expensive looking black combat vest that was exceptionally well organized and replete with items similar to what I carried. His expensive sunglasses were propped up on the top of his head, over his shiny black, gelled back hair. I realized in a few seconds, that this guy must have been a Turkish Special Forces soldier, and I assumed he might have something to do with the contention between the Kurds and the Turkmen.

Neither one of us knew how to react. I thought to myself: is he the enemy? Will he try to kill me? Should I kill him first? How loyal are these Turkmen to this guy? I was sure by the look on the guy's face that he was asking himself a similar set of questions. No one had provided any guidance on what to do if we encountered Turkish Special Forces, or if they did, I hadn't listened. I didn't know what to do, so I smiled broadly and extended my hand to greet him; I had no desire to invoke a firefight with a few hundred armed Turkmen fighters and a team of Turkish Special Forces. He shook my hand and we both realized we were not a threat to each other. The guy spoke English, and we talked about what a mess Iraq was because of all these factions fighting over the scraps of a now broken country. He explained, in general terms, his mission to make sure the deal that the US made with Turkey that promised the Kurds would leave Kirkuk at some point actually happened. I explained our role as well, and that we were waiting to be replaced by US conventional forces.

He was disappointed that his team wasn't in Kirkuk, because Tuz was a side show for them. I deduced that this guy was on a quest for war like I had been, and he wanted to play in the biggest game he could, which was not Tuz. We chatted for a while about each other's weaponry and equipment. I told him about the night we drove into Tuz through a minefield, and he said his experience getting into Tuz was less exciting. We compared rifles and scopes and I asked him how one goes about becoming a Turkish SF soldier, and we compared that to Green Beret training. He seemed like a good guy who was just there to fulfil an expectation and do his job, like I was. He offered to buy me a drink next time I was in Istanbul. We shook hands and jokingly promised not to kill each other once I left, or at least not *intentionally*.[39]

Finally, the conventional forces arrived in APCs. They bumbled through Tuz, and instantly elicited a feeling of unrest from the people there. My Captain handled all the coordination with them. There were also some Marines nearby, but I think they were near Tikrit. The relationship between us and the conventional forces was interesting, and I wasn't very involved in the collaboration personally.

The Kurds provided us with so much information and intelligence, so constantly, that reporting it all, and judging the veracity of it all, became an intractable problem. We attempted to feed the information straight to the conventional troops, but it seemed like they couldn't use intelligence that did not come from their "higher." This meant that they had to wait for our reporting to go up through the echelons and back down for them to actually use it, even though they were *right there with us to begin with*. We sent a note to the Marines near Tikrit, to tell them some of our Kurds were adamantly reporting to us that Sadaam was hiding in Tikrit.[40]

One day, we were told that a former Iraqi officer had information about where WMD might still be located. I was tasked to drive him around to investigate, so I picked him up from my company headquarters, which was in Kirkuk, and he directed me to a certain location on the outskirts of the city. Within a few minutes of conversing via an interpreter, I discovered that the man spoke Spanish; he'd studied it at a university in Baghdad. Since I spoke a bit of Spanish, which I had learned from my Dominican wife, we were able to communicate in equally broken Spanish.

As he gave us directions, we chatted as best we could, using my interpreter frequently as our Spanish skills failed us, about the war and the buildup and everything that had taken place. He asked me if it was true that US Green Berets had to kill a family member as part of their initiation into the Green Berets. He was serious. I laughed and explained to him how silly that was. He said that one of the reasons some of the Iraqi Army units along the Green Line didn't surrender was because they thought the US Green Berets and Kurds would round them all up and kill them. He also explained that another reason some units didn't surrender was because they had no inter communications after the initial Shock and Awe occurred. So, since the Iraqi Army had a very centralized leadership structure, they could not surrender because they could not be communicated to in order to be *told* to surrender.[41]

He directed us to an ordinary building on the outskirts of Kirkuk, and I walked with him in search of the supposed WMD cache. He led me into a dark chamber in the bottom of a building, but nothing was there. He told me it must have been moved along with everything else. Of course, based on his mannerisms, it seemed to me like he was just pulling a stunt to vindicate himself, perhaps to put himself in a good place after the political smoke cleared in Iraq.[42] We brought him back to my Company HQ.

On another seemingly random occasion, I was tasked to escort some Syrian "detainees" all the way up to Mosul. Shortly thereafter, I had three blindfolded and handcuffed Syrians in the land rover headed Northwest. The Syrian men were probably in their thirties, skinny, but in fairly decent condition, and they wore jeans and t-shirts. I had an interpreter with me, and I told them they were not allowed to talk to each other on the way. However, after about an hour, the silence was killing me, so I started asking them "what are you in for" kinds of questions. They said there was a mix up, and they didn't know why they'd been captured. However, they said they were relieved when they'd been taken into custody, because they knew the US Army would provide them a free ride out of Baghdad, which is the only reason they did not deny any accusations; they needed a ride. They said they had operated a fairly successful chocolate store in Baghdad prior to the war, and since the way they were talking and interacting seemed wildly innocent, so I believed them.

I continued questioning them about their lives and what it was like when our military rolled in. They responded with the usual answer; Sadaam was a bastard, but now it's going to get messy. They also laughed about the notion that this war was "over." The relationship in the car escalated quickly, and by the time we got to Mosul several hours later I had learned a few Syrian folk songs, and these men were laughing hysterically as I tried to sing along with them. Of course, since I can't speak or sing Arabic, I'm sure it was hilarious because I had no idea what I was singing, I was just making sounds similar to theirs.

We arrived at the US outpost to turn over the Syrians, and of course I pretended that we hadn't been talking as we pulled into the compound. I stopped the vehicle, and the Syrians said goodbye as they were taken away by some Army personnel.

The chocolate makers were scared to death, and the way they were hauled away so coldly annoyed me greatly. Suddenly, as I watched them walk off, I felt thoroughly fed up with it all, but I couldn't define why. I watched as the Syrians were moved into a white building, and I hoped they walked away thinking "hey, those Americans that gave us a ride were cool." I drove back to Tuz frustrated. [43]

A few weeks later, the conventional units ordered the Kurds to leave Kirkuk. This created a tension that almost caused a catastrophic loss of rapport with the Kurds across my entire unit, which was completely embedded with the Peshmerga all over Northern Iraq. According to the Kurds, they felt like they were being treated like criminals. My team overcame the rapport issue the way Green Berets always do, like I had in Bosnia and Kosovo; by creating the perception that there was clear separation between us and the conventional forces, and any political decisions in general.

Once the Kurds were out of Kirkuk, and some of them left Tuz, we pulled back to get ready to go home. We said our goodbyes to the Kurds over tea, packed up our weapons and equipment, and drove towards As Sulaymaniya. We drove the road of doom one last time, this time stenciling chili peppers on the road at random intervals to leave our mark. Once we got to the Kurdish headquarters, we loaded a Chinook helicopter, and flew towards either Mosul or Irbil, I don't remember which it was.

The helicopter took fire and banked sharply, and the machine gunner in the helicopter returned fire. I winced at the sound and head pounding concussion of the firing, closed my eyes, and asked myself painfully *"when will this end?"* I grew tense and that familiar doomsday feeling swept over me again as I pictured our helicopter getting shot down, and pictured the details of people being shredded, both of which made me yearn for our exfiltration.

After about an hour, we landed, unloaded, and I approached a warehouse-like hangar building. I was very glad to get away from that helicopter. I saw dozens of Green Berets hanging around near the hangar, all telling war stories and waiting to go home. All the other teams were jealous that my team was tasked to do both the AFO mission, *and* we were the main effort on Operation Viking Hammer. Some teams never saw any combat at all, which meant that I was standing amidst a lot of unfulfilled quests for war. After hearing countless descriptions of varying acts of violence and incidents of gore, I became overwhelmed and decided that I didn't want to talk or hear about any of it. A feeling of claustrophobic anxiety swept over me and everything I had seen over the last three months started streaming into my head. It was as if the shield of adrenaline had suddenly disappeared. I started spinning, and I walked away to sit on a bunk away from everyone else in the corner of the hangar.

My mind churned uncontrollably as I sat on the bunk. I thought about how this quest for war had kept me away from my family in Connecticut for so many years, and how much strain this lifestyle I had chosen affected my wife and mother. My wife and I have a special way that we shake hands with each other that we invented on our first date, and I yearned for that touch. I laid down and grew more and more frustrated with myself as I questioned every choice I had ever made in my life. Subconsciously, I began to wonder if I had ever really been who I thought I was or who I had always tried to be. If I wasn't who I

119

thought I was all those years on my quest for war, then who was I now that the quest is over? I was disappointed in myself because my mind was such a mess over it all; I was supposed to be a "badass Green Beret," but I sure didn't feel like one, and I didn't think I had really performed like one. I hadn't expected this new experience with *real* war to suddenly affect me so much.

I just laid there with my eyes closed and body completely tensed. I listened to the intense ringing in my ears and involuntarily re-experienced the noises and images of war that streamed through my conscience and drowned out the world around me. Suddenly, I could not stop the accumulation of visualizations that rushed through my visual memory, from Bosnia, Kosovo, and what I had just seen in Iraq. In my mind's eye, it was like the images of war had amassed and were attacking me. I felt like the guy in *A Clockwork Orange* with his eyelids forced open to watch horrific videos against his will, except the videos were in my own mind. [44]

Before I knew it we had flown across the Atlantic and landed at Peterson Air Force base in Colorado Springs. We drove a bus back to our team room at Ft Carson, unloaded our stuff, locked our guns away, said our goodbyes, and headed home. It was no different than any other day when we came back to the team room after a random day of training.

I walked through the parking lot to my truck and freaked out for a second because I no longer had a weapon in my hands. As I drove through Ft Carson I realized that I had forgotten where I lived. I felt like an alien who had just landed on another planet. I pulled over and had to think about it for a while. I was finally able to concentrate long enough to get oriented and remember where I lived, and I headed over the Interstate 25 overpass; my ears were ringing like crazy and my mind was massively distracted in an indefinable way. I had no idea what I was going to say to my wife when I walked in the door. She had flown back out to Colorado with my daughter to meet me.

My mind was still pegged on primitive fears and visions of horror, and my nerves were still electrified from a severe case of permanent alarm. So, although I wanted to go home and act like I never left, I couldn't even convince myself that I was *safe*.

I was overwhelmed when I saw my wife, because there were so many times I thought I might not ever see her again. My daughter looked totally different even though I had only been gone about five months. I am a very anti-emotional person, I guess I'm a typical rural Connecticut swamp Yankee, so I didn't break down and cry when we embraced. I hugged my wife and daughter and I was flooded with so many different emotions I went emotionally numb. My daughter didn't feel well, she was crying a lot, and thankfully her crying took the focus off the fact that I had just gotten home from war. Of course, my wife asked me "how was it?" and I really couldn't aggregate the enormity of what I had just seen into a concise answer, so I said "everything went ok." My wife kept looking into my eyes, as if she was looking for something she was used to seeing and it wasn't there anymore. I didn't realize how much what I had just seen in Iraq had disturbed and impacted me.

Now

After OVH, and the war, my life took an interesting turn. I shifted my focus to my family. I became an 18F intelligence instructor, which led to me ultimately becoming a technology professional in the Big Data, Analytics, and Software Engineering space. I retired in 2011 as an E8, and now I am a Senior Director in a technology company.

The one thing that OVH taught me more than anything, or confirmed, is the power of Green Berets. When combined with AFSOC and CIA, conducting Unconventional Warfare, the teams are unstoppable. Two battalions of Green Berets, a handful of CIA and AFSOC, along with the Kurds and some air support, took down three terrorist groups, and then defeated (or dispersed) 2/3 of the Iraqi Army. The cost of sending Green Berets is not much more than the men's salaries, weapons, and transportation, and we usually fly commercial air. Think of the sustainability aspect. Also, since we are embedded with indigenous forces, our intelligence is hyper localized and in real time. We are cheaper and massively more effective for unconventional warfare against emerging extremist groups. Perhaps OVH should be considered a model for success in modern warfare.

The End

Follow my on Quora, or connect with me on LinkedIN for direct feedback any time

Chapter 5
Introspections

1   Officers: Never underestimate how much your people rely on you. The degree to which your troops will trust you is unimaginable: don't violate that trust. For the most part during this whole infiltration journey, which I was wildly ignorant to what the consequences would be if we were captured, I was simply doing what I was told. It was with absolute and unquestionable trust that I observed my Captain coordinate anything that needed to be coordinated and then disseminate orders; I trusted him with my life more than I trusted myself with my life.

2   As part of the pre mission training that my unit had organized prior to our deployment, my Battalion commander and his staff brought in some cultural experts from top universities to give us several briefings on the history of the Kurds and the region in general. This was immensely helpful in developing an accurate perception of the situation we were in. I often wonder why the government doesn't rely on the academic community more to produce highly informed situational awareness. In hindsight I wish I'd had the same education before going to Kosovo, I wish I would have listened more, and had the intellect to fully digest what they were telling us.

3   From a Green Beret "Unconventional Warfare" enthusiast perspective, this was love at first site. I thought I was about to have my own rag-bag guerillas just like all those Green Berets in all those Vietnam books I had read.

4   later in life when I entered the world of the intelligence community, I was never able to find a single one of those reports...the information seemed to have vaporized.

5   Waiting for those jets to attack was one of the first times in war that I felt a feeling of total helplessness, combined with a feeling of impending doom. This feeling is like the electric feeling one feels when someone severely startles you, except in war this feeling does not go away almost instantly; it lingers and radiates. It is like being in a permanent state of severely startled or alarmed. If those jets were

---

coming to bomb us, then there was absolutely nothing I could have done about it.

[6]   At this time in northern Iraq it was nothing like the average American can understand or even imagine. Ansar Al Islam, IGK, and IMK, which were all violent extremist groups, had established areas that they explicitly marked, declared ownership of, and protected with bands of armed militants, landmines, machine gun bunkers, and whatever else they could. The three groups did not exactly get along, but they shared the PUK as a common enemy. Imagine the town next to yours suddenly becoming an autonomous radicalized area, a place where if you drove to the supermarket you could be decapitated by extremists and end up with your head on a stake (literally), or you would encounter a machine gun bunker in the road manned by armed militia and be forced to turn back. They flew their flags blatantly, they dug trenches and built machine gun positions around their areas, and they had foreign fighters from all over the radical "Islamic" world training and fighting there. This is the real world outside of your cul de sac.

[7]   To this day, my entire body tenses up uncontrollably at the thought of that sound, it is supernatural in character. One major lesson this incident taught me was how insignificant I felt while at the mercy of that mortar round. When it was screaming through that huge sky towards me, totally invisible, there was absolutely nothing I could do to change where it might land, like shooting a bow straight up and having no control where the arrow will come down. Again, it was the next level of that feeling of helplessness mixed with a sense of impending doom that I had felt before, and all I could do was hope I don't die or become irreversibly mangled. It didn't matter one bit when that mortar was flying towards me that I was a Green Beret and an Airborne Ranger and a Sniper and a whatever. In fact, none of my training mattered at all at that instant because that mortar was either going to "get" me or it wasn't. This was the beginning of establishing in my mind one of the things I hate most about war; nothing you have ever done in life matters in the face of war, you are at its mercy, it reduces you to a primitive animal. Sure, as a soldier you can be cunning in your planning, and creative in your strategies and techniques, and a master of your tools, but when it comes time to face off against other humans, and munitions are flying, you either make it or you don't, and nothing you've ever done in your life is going to change that. It's just plain not fair. Not to mention, the whole idea of

taking out a leader of one of these extremist networks is really ineffectual anyway, so the whole recon was pointless. How did we think we were going to identify a leader among these AAI fighters? Longer beard?

8   The Peshmerga were generally fatalistic in nature, meaning they did not think much in life was really within their control, so our planning seemed very academic to them. They use the phrase "Inshallah" a lot. Inshallah (poor transliteration maybe) can be best translated as "if God is willing," and based on my experience with its context I would say it actually more specifically means "only if God is willing." So when they were told that they had to secure a hill by a certain time, their response would be "inshallah," and they really refused to have much confidence in being able to promise anything would happen at a specific time or other details that might be situationally dependent. They instead relied on simple plans and dynamic decision making to accomplish most tasks. I actually respected their refusal to create absolutes; it ties in rather well with my own theory that war has a way of placing you at its mercy.

9   Only in the Green Berets does a Major or Captain find himself responsible for a ten-thousand-man attack that is critical to the success of a national strategic campaign, and only in the Green Berets does an E6 or E7 find himself in a role similar to a battalion commander, integrating airpower into hundreds or thousands of indigenous fighters. This is what makes the Green Berets special. Being part of this operation was surreal at the time, I had trained for about 12 years prior, and this was the culmination of my quest for war. Also, our level of integration with the CIA was interesting, we got along quite well, not like you see in some movies

10   The Kurds taught us that if you hard-mount a machine gun to a vehicle, you are now tied to that vehicle, and you will instantly become a magnet for every enemy munition within range as soon as you fire it. They recommended that we just throw the big guns (.50 cal and the MK19) in the back of the trucks along with their tripods; this way, we could take out the gun, set it up anywhere that afforded some protection, and use it without being completely exposed on the top of a light skinned vehicle. This was counter intuitive to us, because the guns look much cooler when they are mounted on vehicles.

11   I don't think there is an equivalent emotion or sentiment within the human spirit that can elicit the same kind of fear as when you realize you are facing other humans who want to kill you. I have done my best to describe this feeling adequately, but it is truly beyond words, its gravity can only be obtained by experience. Philosophically, when I think about the whole situation in hindsight, it is very interesting how so intensely duty bound both sides were that day. In fact, my own underpinning logic that what I was doing was important and totally necessary (whether true or not) was unconquerable...no one could have convinced me otherwise at that time. I just thought what we were doing was the right thing to do.... eliminating terrorists.... which also has many more layers that I didn't see then.

12   It's also difficult to convey in writing how when one suddenly faces death, how refined and primitive one's thinking becomes. Survival instinct must be at the core of how I became like an animal, keen in all my senses, sagacious in all my movements, head clear of all worldly distractions. I realized later, this primordial clearing of one's head to focus on survival for prolonged periods of time is what makes it hard to psychologically recover from war; to readapt to a world where other-than-survival actually matters is really hard, and it's so primitive that it's not a function of logic, so it's hard to command.

13   When I think about that instant as we neared Gulp, I often reflect on the way the Peshmerga operated. They flowed through mountains like a large adaptive and self-organizing horde. When any piece of the horde is engaged, a contingent of appropriate size ("appropriate" is determined instantly based on instinct) is dispatched to eliminate that threat. A new element of the horde then takes to the front, and the horde continues to move forward, never stopping, never pausing, ever; a purely offensive approach to combat. Most of the elements within the horde were likely based on hometown, tribe, or even possibly by family. Radios were in short supply, so separation into many smaller groups would have made communication impossible. When the Peshmerga were in battle, they reminded me of life forms that have swarm intelligence; like bees, ants, or when starlings swarm in the sky. They move like a single dynamic adaptive system, and don't need much more than a general direction and a desired end-state to make things happen. There was beauty in their method; fast, agile, simple, and brutally effective. It was really

pointless that any of us even carried guns when we were integrated with the Peshmerga. In fact, now I think it was pointless that the US ever deployed conventional troops to Iraq at all, given that the Green Berets of the 10th Special Forces Group (and some from 3rd Group and AFSOC) had collectively organized over one hundred thousand Kurds who would have gone anywhere with us. I wonder what would have happened in Iraq if we'd taken a purely Unconventional, Surrogate warfare approach?

[14] Combat is massively frustrating. It's not like the movies where people instantly identify who is shooting at them, and then they easily take them out. I couldn't see anything, and when the bullets are flying you can't just stand up and look around to find who's shooting at you. There is dust, sweat in your eyes, fog on your glasses, you're out of breath, the bad guys are moving, you're moving, and you have to stay behind cover. This moment outside Gulp is probably when I subconsciously started to realize that this battle wasn't going to be as glorious and straight forward as my daydreams about war had been over the 12 years prior. Also, in hindsight I really didn't think my vision was very good, and you'll see why if you read the whole book.

[15] This was the first human I killed. I had wounded people in Kosovo, and I had killed AAI with mortars from a distance, but this was more personal. At the time it didn't feel much different than today when I fill out a timecard or drive through the EZ-Pass lane; part of my job. However, nowadays I continuously contemplate it, morally and philosophically, and I think about how all the events prior led up to that particular instance in time that pitted that guy and I against each other; radicalization, regime change, subjective philosophy, politics, survival, definitions of morality and justness in the world, evil, threats to the homeland, invasion...I find it all interesting

[16] Again, as a writer I did my best to convey this scene's intensity, and although I believe my depiction is cogent, it still does not correlate with the images in my own memory. No analogy to anything in everyday life transfers, no amount of wordsmithing suffices. The noise was that of a thousand airplanes, or perhaps standing in the middle of a highway pileup with a thousand airplanes flying low overhead, or perhaps all of the above plus having someone punching you in the face while meteors strike the earth around you.

The intensity was god-like. The phrase "War is Hell" always seemed cliché to me, but now I can fully contextualize it.

17   Again, here I learned just how difficult it is to locate the enemy when you're in a battle like this. Everything is moving everywhere; they're moving, you're moving, dust is flying, and since you're receiving fire you can't safely look anywhere long enough to identify anything, and as soon as you think you spot an enemy you will need to take cover again. Of course, when you pop back up from the cover, you find that everything has changed all over again, and the cycle continues. It's maddening, especially when you add fear to the equation.

18   The debates about only needing to meet some minimal standard to get into combat units makes me reflect on this moment. The men on my team were physically invincible. "Olympians with guns" is not a hyperbolic term. To special operators, the minimum standard is irrelevant. It is considered a criterion for failure; merely a gate for the initial training. What matters more than minimal standards is the true potential of a team; what the team can attain together as a group and as individuals. Teams of men have a way of intra-competing their way to incredibly high standards, pushing each other to incredible heights, and I can't help but think that throwing someone in the mix that can, at best, barely exceed some minimal standard should be unacceptable because it undermines this natural tendency to maximize group potential. Why don't women and men compete with each other in the Olympics? Why don't the Olympics have a minimal standard for entry? Why don't WNBA and NBA teams compete against each other? The answers are easy: potential is what really matters, not opportunity, and potential is stifled by the forced placement of a weak link, but bolstered by truly challenging intra-team competition. Just because someone can pass an initial entry test to attempt a training course, or barely pass a school that has become marginally rigorous, does not mean the long-term potential to achieve awesomeness will still be there for the whole team. I am not a macho kind of guy at all, please don't put the book down now because you think that's what I am. I am totally the opposite and very compassionate, but this one is a no brainer to me. Realistically though, on the other hand as a counterpoint, as a nation we have to balance keeping high standards, and actually filling the ranks, so although my

little theory of potential is great, it is not necessarily holistic nor pragmatic.

[19]   In hindsight, I don't think our removal of that AAI machine gun was as important as the motivation that we provided by being up there firing that big .50 cal machine gun. A .50 cal tends to speak a universal language, and it can become a motivational speaker if it's on your side. I think what this action really gave everyone was a sense of security, possibly a false sense of security. Regardless, this sense of security gave us all motivation and courage, and that's what we needed more than anything at that point. Maybe there is an important strategic lesson here...sometimes something that creates a perception or changes a mindset can make a difference just because of the way it affects people psychologically, which can often make certain other actions "work" even though the action itself isn't so amazing.

[20]   I learned as an SF weapons Sergeant that you shouldn't fire more than a few rounds per day out of a 106 because it can actually separate the sac of skin from around your heart due to so much concussive power. That didn't apply this day.

[21]   I previously mentioned Bafel, but it's important to know his significance. Bafel Talibani is the son of Jalal Talibani, the future president of Iraq and the leader of the PUK. He is a very significant figure in the Kurdish Peshmerga leadership. Google him and his dad Jalal to learn more. He's a heck of a leader and a fighter, and a really nice guy with a dashing British accent.

[22]   There were so few of us, and so many Kurds, and they moved so dynamically that it was nearly impossible to account for where they could be at any given time. Trying to keep track of where they all were was an intractable task; the best approach was to try to stay on the front line with them at all times and spread out among them, but that was not easy to accomplish in reality when the "front line" is measured in miles, and it's not straight. This is one of the challenges in unconventional warfare using surrogate forces: "command and control" turns into an exercise of continuous accountability, but with unsophisticated communications.

[23]   This was the first instance of the feeling I refer to later in the book as "total body shutdown." I never felt like this in my life until this

day, and the feeling frequently recurs ever since. No doctor has ever been able to explain it to me.

24   If any officers are reading this, it is really important for you to realize how much your interaction with soldiers means to them. It's not just the status of the rank, established by military protocol; it is more about the character and personality you display. Most soldiers are uneducated and don't formulate ideas in a structured and overtly logical way (sorry), but they are cunning and very perceptive for the most part, which gives them great bullshit identification skills. Be authentic, have an opinion, be open minded, be consistent, be one step better than them physically and mentally, and stay genuine; if you don't, they will merely pretend to trust and respect you out of obligation, and fear of the military justice system.

25   I have thought about what had happened to this guy's head and face ever since, and I have concluded that maybe he was hit in the face by a flying large rock that was thrown from a blast. It's also possible that perhaps he was wounded, and the Kurds smashed his face in with the buttstock of a weapon or by stomping it in. Visions like this stay vivid forever.

26   Try to imagine cutting hair off of dead people that are shredded and burnt to a crisp, or next time you see a particularly nasty roadkill, pull over, walk over to it, touch it, cut some hair off it, and then pretend it's human. The images of this scene haunt me worse and worse over the years as the memories become more analyzed in my continuously-opening mind.

27   Years later, after I had become part of the intelligence community for a while, around 2007 I think it was, people were acting like they'd made a grand discovery that there were "foreign fighters" coming into Iraq, which is a testament to how temporal and transient knowledge is in the intel world.

28   This situation exposes a key challenge in counter terrorism...the perception that going after them will actually do any good or not; and opinions vary (rightfully so). These terrorists don't have a nationality, they follow no laws, borders don't exist to them, and they can easily melt into the population. So, direct attacks on them aren't always very effective long term, they just cause

dispersion, morphing, reorganization, then reemergence. I talk about this enough in other parts of the book. Whack a mole as a military tactic is certainly unsustainable, but often the only option (if one feels compelled to do anything at all). What would have happened if we had never routed AAI? Would they have built something horrible in the Sargat facility? Would they have faded away? Would AQI and ISIS have formed if AAI hadn't been dispersed? I imagine Bob Dylan could probably tell us where these answers are (blowing in the wind).

29   Our greatest contributions to the Peshmerga efforts were that we bolstered their ability to communicate with each other over large distances, which enabled the ability to synchronize large scale attacks. The other obvious contribution was that we integrated air power. The Kurds needed zero help from us to fight discrete ground battles, they needed help via air support and communications. It only took a tiny amount of Green Berets to make the Peshmerga a world class fighting force, a force that I believe could have accomplished the entirety of the Iraq war in half the time, at a fraction of the cost, and with significantly less long term side effects (assuming we should have been in Iraq at all in the first place).

30   I actually thought we may stumble into "the WMD" and be the heroes of the war. I had no idea how complicated the situation really was, how huge the country of Iraq was, all the possibilities that Sadaam may have moved or distributed the materials (if they existed at all), and it didn't occur to me that it all might have been completely unfounded. Was it? Likely, no one will ever know, because it's impossible to "know." Also, the Kurds assured us that if any WMD had ever been anywhere then the politics we played for 8 months prior to invading had given Sadaam plenty of time to get the stuff hidden. They actually thought it was kind of a joke that we even asked about it; they laughed at the idea. However, they assumed that Sadaam did indeed have WMD, because he used it on the Kurds back in 88 in Halabja; they had no reason to believe he'd just stop making it. How do you know when you know or don't know something? If you're not sure, should you act preemptively just in case, or should you wait for more information with more veracity? How long do you wait? What degree of veracity must be attained? How do you measure veracity? These questions tie directly into whether or not you think the invasion of Iraq in 2003 was just or not.

31   Interestingly, and it's counterintuitive, when you are a Special Forces team, embedded with the Indigenous fighters, and you are not a member of the multi-billion dollar, three-star-General-led tank brigades headed to Baghdad, you don't get priority air support. We only got air support in the form of what our Air Force guy called "ash and trash," which meant we only got support randomly from jets and bombers that were flying back from their missions over Baghdad and other points south. So we basically had to just wait for some pilot to fly over that had some extra munitions we could put to use. This also meant that if we came under massive contact from the overwhelming force of Iraqis in front of us then we had no guarantee of getting timely air support.

32   There are points in time where things become clear, where the smoke settles and we can see with specificity. This was the point that I started to see that I was having some issues with what was happening. I knew that I was doing my job, and we weren't doing anything unlawful in terms of war, but it was at a deeper level that I was questioning it all. War is universally troubling to the soul, regardless of context, especially given time to contemplate it.

33   Knowing the Green Beret Officer Corps the way I do now in hindsight, I am confident that my senior leaders were very well aware and probably thinking the same thing way before I did.

34   It is interesting how children have a predilection to desire niceness in people, and how in the face of this almost universal trait among children we adults still find a way to perpetuate things like hate and war. That little girl had hope in her eyes, hope for nothing more than that I would turn out to be nice.

35   I think I know now, that we had basically just created the wild west. Was Sadaam's brutality the only thing that kept Iraq together the years prior to our invasion? If so, was regime change such a good idea? Also, was it regime change, or regime removal? Change implies transition, removal implies suddenness, and suddenness is usually accompanied by a shock, and shock instantiates desperation, and desperation causes widespread seizure of opportunity by any means.

36   Most people don't realize it, because it's counter-intuitive, but Green Berets are trained to "build rapport" with indigenous

people as one of their core competencies. It is actually a skill that is held in very high regard (or at least it was when I was in SF.) In fact, in Special Forces Assessment and Selection (SFAS), the "team week" torture test was all about how well you can get along with people under stress. Green Berets all go to language school as well, which, due to enabling direct communications, makes them more effective at building rapport with locals and host nation militaries. If you are a Green Beret or want to be one, do not think that language school is a waste of time, it is incredibly important. Being proficient in language is not as cool as wearing Oakleys on the firing range with your sleeves rolled up, but it is actually way more useful than most of your other "combat" training in my experience.

37   In hindsight, I have to question everything I thought I knew at the time. Had we bombed IGK for no reason or was this guy lying? If IGK was such a savage radical group, why was this guy even willing to talk to me? Likely survival. The Kurds gave us information during our AFO mission that IGK was helping AAI, but was that information true, or had the Kurds just manipulated us to secure more territory? Did we have other information I wasn't aware of? Also, this was a confusing time. The war was declared over, but the war with who? Only with the Iraqi army, or was it over for "terrorist" groups as well? Was IGK a terrorist group? At the time, I understood the war being "over" to mean we weren't supposed to attack anyone anymore, but it wasn't actually clear. Maybe we shouldn't have talked to them at all, and instead planned an attack?

38   When we returned back to Colorado, the proud owners of the Western Omelet had framed and hung our picture on the wall in the restaurant. ODA 081 would be forever remembered. I seem to remember that some patrons to the restaurant thought that the picture glorified war, and it should be taken down. At the time I remember feeling surprised that anyone would think like that, but after I have thought about war for ten years, and studied ethics, I understand this viewpoint now, even though I don't agree with it.

39   Again, in war, soldiers take actions based on what their respective "higher powers" expect of them, which is often contrary to what actions our natural human tendencies might have otherwise prescribed. Sounds cliché, but War really does paradoxically show us the absolute worst and best of the human spirit.

40   This was 2003, and Tikrit is where we captured Sadaam many years later...I can't help but wonder what would have happened if they would have listened to us and captured him then (if he was actually there). Would the war have dragged on for so many years?

41   The power of propaganda and military bureaucracy is often stunning on a galactic scale. It's amazing what people will believe when their information environment is controlled and manipulated by a higher power. Imagine if what this guy said was true...that the only reason they didn't surrender is because they couldn't be told to surrender. What if they had surrendered and become Iraqi security forces?

42   He wanted to be perceived as a team player, and this was his attempt to make it obvious. One has to be very careful in Unconventional Warfare...everyone has an agenda, and they will play any games they can to influence their way into a good position within the chaos so once the smoke clears they can find themselves in a better place. There were several occasions when local Kurds claimed that certain other groups were involved with nefarious activity in order to try and elicit our air support, when in actuality the other group may have been just a competitor for territory and resources in the area. Navigating these kinds of problems in Unconventional Warfare is probably similar to being caught in the middle of rival Mafia group activities. Dealing with things like this actually transferred fairly well to the business world later on.

43   In hindsight, I think the humanity in me might have been trying to fend off the reality of the environment I was in and the horrors I had just experienced. I wanted to say, "hey, these dudes are just chocolate makers trying to get a ride out of Baghdad because we just destroyed it... just let 'em go."

44   I was confused at a primitive emotional level that day as I sat on that cot, and these emotions were totally indefinable to me then. Prior to this moment, I assumed I had been sent to Iraq for good reason. I assumed the battle against AAI had been worth it. I assumed the regime change was the right move. Today, as I look back on these experiences in Iraq my emotions are just as confused as the myriad interpretations and opinions that still proliferate about it all.

Regarding my efforts against AAI, I tend to think our actions were just, but it doesn't really matter if the actions were just or not, because I don't think our actions were very impactful. Some will say terrorists like Ansar Al Islam, and ISIS, need to be attacked and killed, while others say that if you do attack them then you've given them what they want: legitimacy. Some say if you attack them their recruiting will increase so it's best to ignore them until they fade away, while others say that if we ignore them, they won't always fade away, and their numbers would eventually increase anyway so we should strike them immediately. Some say that they hate us for what we are, not what we do, so leaving them alone won't work for that reason alone. Some speculate that they will attack us at home, while others don't think they can. Some say we have to go "hyper local" to defeat extremists, but that has huge resourcing problems. Some say you can't kill ideology, you can only affect it indirectly, and it can pop up anywhere. So, given all this disparate thought, I have concluded that we are caught in a conundrum: attack and bolster their recruiting, or do nothing and hope that they will eventually lose interest knowing they might grow stronger. Either way, the occasional ideologically driven lunatic will inevitably attack us. We certainly can't mass kill as a means of routing them because innocent people will die and that is morally and politically unacceptable and would of course massively drive up global recruitment. However, cherry picking as a war strategy -trying to fight a war like a giant police investigation, AKA, whack a mole- faces massive scalability problems and leads to imminent failure because they will just fade into the population and wait until we leave, and we will spend billions of dollars and lose thousands of lives pointlessly playing whack-a-mole for decades. I have thought about these opinions and my own obsessively, grappling with whether or not what I went through was really worth going through. Was it worth it? Now I tend to be in the camp that thinks if you denounce them, and keep your distance while letting other local nations deal with it, it erodes their cause, which makes them less attractive to the pools of troubled souls in the world that they recruit from. You can't permanently stop dedicated nut jobs of any kind, but you can stop making more of them; but in some cases you just have to schwack em even if you know it's temporary. Modern warfare is difficult, I'm glad we weren't so constrained back in WWII.

Printed in Great Britain
by Amazon